T0316996

Crochet Motif Book

366 DAYS
CROCHET MOTIFS

AN ESSENTIAL COLLECTION FEATURING
SQUARE, FLORAL, CIRCULAR, LACY MOTIFS, AND MORE

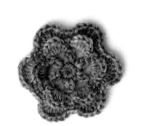

Tuva

Contents

Crochet Motifs

Projects

Technique Guide

Materials and Tools

We introduce yarns and basic tools you will need when crocheting motifs.

Yarn: Crochet and Lace Weight Yarn

The size and impression of the finished motif can vary depending on the yarn used, even with the same crochet chart. Imagine the finished product and enjoy crocheting motifs with various materials and shapes such as wool, mohair, cotton, silk, and gradient colors.

Lace yarn is denoted by numbers such as "20, 30...," and the higher the number, the thinner the yarn becomes.

Motifs on pages 8-79

Puppy New 4PLY
(medium-fine type, using 2.25mm to 2.50mm hooks)

Motifs on pages 80-115

Olympus Emmy Grande
(lace weight yarn, using 1.75mm to 1.50mm hooks)

Crochet & Lace Hooks

Crochet Hooks: Crochet hooks are labeled as "2.00, 2.25mm" and the larger the number, the thicker the shaft of the hook.

Lace Hooks: Lace hooks are labeled as "1.75, 1.50" and the larger the number, the finer the tip of the hook.

Scissors

We recommend craft scissors with thin blades that cut well.

Yarn Needles

Used for finishing off and weaving in yarn ends. Choose the needle size according to the thickness of the yarn and the intended use.

Yarns Used in This Book

(The photos are in actual size.)

We used the following yarns for the motifs, wearables and accessories featured in this book. The same motif (Motif 4 / Page 8) is crocheted with each yarn. Please use it as a reference for the size and texture of the motifs when crocheting your own.

1. Puppy New 4PLY
100% Wool (Superwash)
40g ball, approx. 150m, 2.00 - 2.30 mm hooks

2. Puppy Cotton Kona Fine
100% Cotton
25g ball, approx. 105m, 1.75 - 2.00 mm hooks

3. Puppy Leafy
100% Non-classified fiber (Paper)
40g ball, approx. 170m, 4.00 - 5.00 mm hooks

4. Olympus Emmy Grande
100% Cotton
50g ball, approx. 218m, 1.75 - 2.00 mm hooks

5. Diamond Masterseed Cotton (Crochet)
100% Cotton
30g ball, approx. 142m, 2.00 - 2.25 mm hooks

6. Ski Tasmanian Polwarth
100% Wool
40g ball, approx. 134m, 3.00 - 3.50 mm hooks

7. Hamanaka Wash Cotton (Crochet)
64% Cotton, 36% Polyester
25g ball, approx. 104m, 2.25 mm hook

8. Hamanaka Paume Baby Color (Crochet)
100% Cotton (Pure Organic Cotton)
25g ball, approx. 110m, 2.25 mm hook

Basics of Crochet

Before starting to crochet, it's important to know the basic knowledge and techniques that are common to all motifs.

▪ Reading Crochet Charts

All crochet symbol charts are presented from the right side. You begin with a foundation chain or magic ring at the center and work outward.

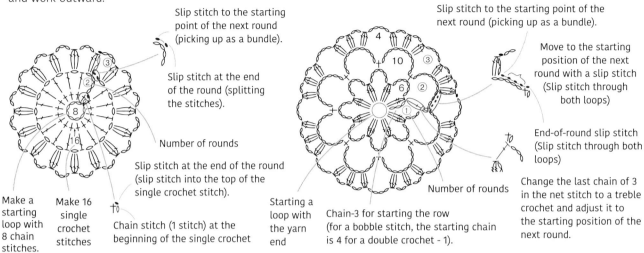

Slip stitch to the starting point of the next round (picking up as a bundle).

Slip stitch at the end of the round (splitting the stitches).

Number of rounds

Slip stitch at the end of the round (slip stitch into the top of the single crochet stitch).

Make a starting loop with 8 chain stitches.

Make 16 single crochet stitches

Chain stitch (1 stitch) at the beginning of the single crochet

Slip stitch to the starting point of the next round (picking up as a bundle).

Move to the starting position of the next round with a slip stitch (Slip stitch through both loops)

End-of-round slip stitch (Slip stitch through both loops)

Change the last chain of 3 in the net stitch to a treble crochet and adjust it to the starting position of the next round.

Starting a loop with the yarn end

Number of rounds

Chain-3 for starting the row (for a bobble stitch, the starting chain is 4 for a double crochet - 1).

Note: Pick up as a bundle. Insert the hook into the space below the stitches of the previous row (mainly chains) and work the stitches by wrapping around them.

Note: To further enlarge the bobble stitch, you might also crochet the same number of starting chains as the bobble stitch.

▪ Foundation Chain

 Magic Ring:
This method tightens the center of the motif. After completing the first round, tighten the yarn end.

 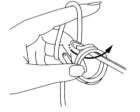   

Tighten

1 Wrap the yarn around your finger twice, then remove the loop from your finger.

2 Hold the intersection and insert the hook into the loop, pulling the yarn through.

3 Wrap the yarn around the hook and pull through.

4 The loop is now created (this loop is not counted as a stitch).

5 After completing the first row, pull the loops from the ball side of the loop one by one, and finally pull the yarn end to tighten the center loop.

 Creating A Loop With Chain Stitches:
This method creates a motif with an open center design. Adjust the size of the center space of the motif by the number of chain stitches used to make the loop.

 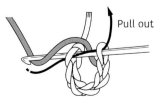 

Pull out

1 After crocheting the necessary number of chains, insert the hook into the first chain stitch.

2 Wrap the yarn around the hook and pull it through.

3 The loop with chain stitches is now complete.

▪ Finishing Crochet

The beginning and end of rows are joined with slip stitches. While the end of a motif is represented by a slip stitch symbol, using a yarn needle provides a neater finish.

End of Row Crochet

Insert the hook into the first stitch. If the first stitch is a single crochet, insert the hook into the top of the single crochet. If it's not a single crochet, insert the hook through the back loop of the turning chain.

The beginning of the row is...

Single Crochet
Pick up the front and back loops of the chain and pull through.

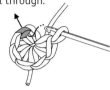

Double Crochet
Pick up the back loop of the chain stitch and pulling through.

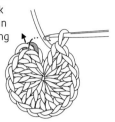

Finishing Off the Motif and Weaving in the Yarn Ends

To connect to the first stitch of the row, use a yarn needle to make one chain stitch.

Weave the yarn end through the stitches on the backside of the motif for about 3-4 cm, and then cut the yarn.

Finishing Off
Pull the last stitch through, leaving a tail of yarn about 7-8 cm long. Thread the yarn onto a yarn needle. Insert the needle into the stitch next to the beginning stitch, then bring the needle back to the center of the last stitch. Pull the yarn through the loop to create a chain stitch.

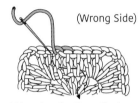

(Wrong Side)

Weaving in Yarn Ends
Turn the motif to the wrong side and weave the yarn end through the stitches to secure it.

For Net Stitch

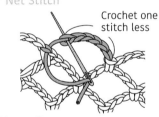

Crochet one stitch less

Finishing Off
For the last net stitch, crochet one chain stitch less than usual, then thread the yarn end onto a yarn needle. Insert the needle under the first two single crochet stitches at the beginning, then bring the needle back to the center of the last chain stitch and make one chain stitch.

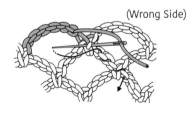

(Wrong Side)

Weaving in Yarn Ends
Turn the motif to the wrong side and weave the yarn end through the stitches to secure it.

▪ Changing Yarn Colors

Change to the next color of yarn when making the slip stitch at the end of the round.

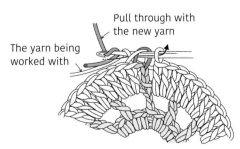

Pull through with the new yarn

The yarn being worked with

Insert the hook the front to the back, then crochet with the new yarn.

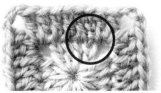

Minimal color change

Color change made during the slip stitch.

Prominent color change

Color change made after the slip stitch.

Simple Motifs

These simple motifs consist of basic stitches such as chain stitch, single crochet, half double crochet, and double crochet. The pattern repeats are also straightforward and easy to remember, allowing you to crochet them anytime and anywhere during your free time.

1, 5/ The first round creates a circular motif, which transforms into a square motif in the second round. Pay attention to the stitches at the corners.

2/ While adjusting the height of the stitches in the third round, ensure that the size of the heads remains consistent.

3, 4/ Like a small cogwheel, this motif can be enjoyed by using different colors and yarn type.

6/ Crochet tightly with single crochet stitches to create a stable and sturdy motif.

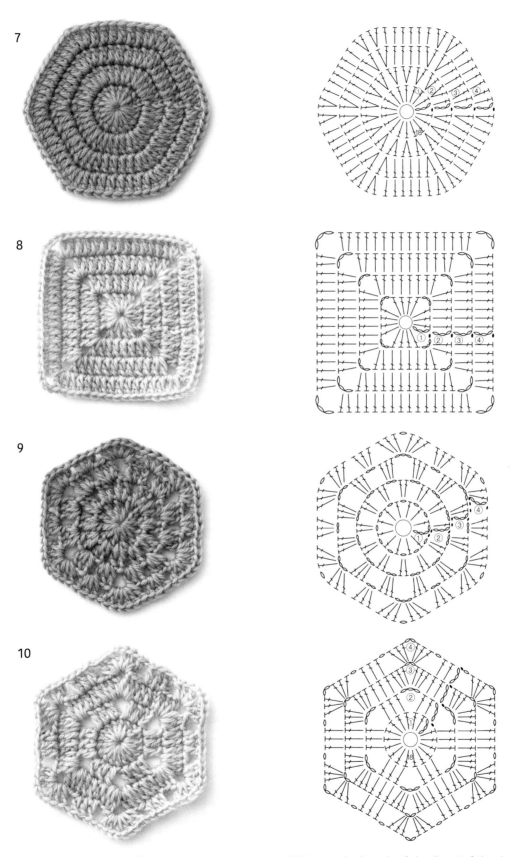

7

8

9

10

7, 10/ Be mindful of the corners of the hexagon as you crochet. The key is to make 18 dc into the magic ring.

8/ Ensure the length of the "legs" of the double crochet stitches crocheted into the magic ring is securely fastened.

9/ A simple and easy-to-understand pattern.

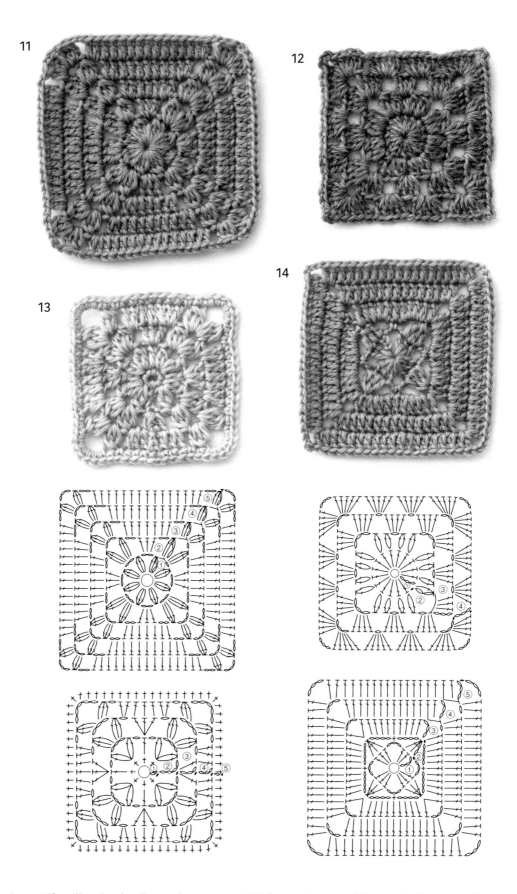

11/ Connecting the motifs will make the diagonal popcorn stitch lines stand out.

12/ The so-called granny-style motif.

13/ The center resembles a cute flower and is recommended for experimenting with color combinations.

14/ It is important to align the double crochet stitches patiently.

15/ When crocheting, ensure that the starting point of the double crochet stitches matches the size of the chain stitches.

16, 18/ Simple patterns that are versatile and applicable to various projects.

17/ Resembles a spinning windmill? Suitable for drawstring bags or purses.

Square Motifs

Square motifs offers incredible versatility, allowing for seamless expansion both vertically and horizontally. Within the simple framework & plethora of patterns awaits- from classic grids and nets to delicate flowers and dynamic mixes. There are plenty of variations!

19/ When working the continuous double crochet stitches, pay attention to aligning the "legs" neatly.

20/ The delicate pattern of small flower petals at the center is charming.

21/ Interesting effects can be made with color combinations.

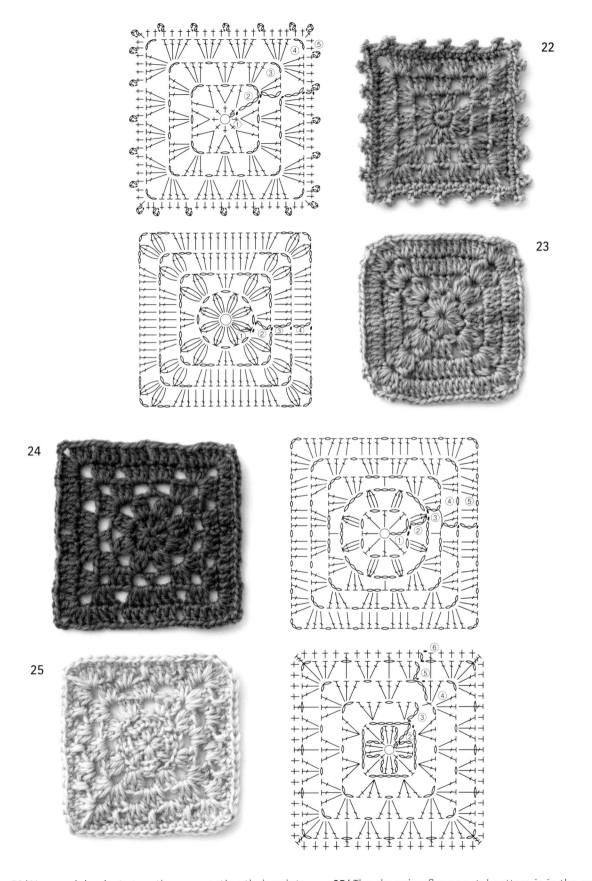

22/ You can join picots together, connecting their points.

23/ A rounded square with two chains at each corner.

24/ Adjust from a circular to a square motif by using double crochet stitches in the third round.

25/ The charming flower petal pattern is in the center. Pay attention to the tension of the long double crochet stitches at the corners.

26/ A motif you'd like to experiment with using different colors and materials.

27/ It's interesting how the squares overlap as they change direction.

28/ A sturdy finish is achieved by using tight single crochet stitches in the final round.

29/ It is possible to vary the lenghs of the "legs" in double crochet and half double crochet.

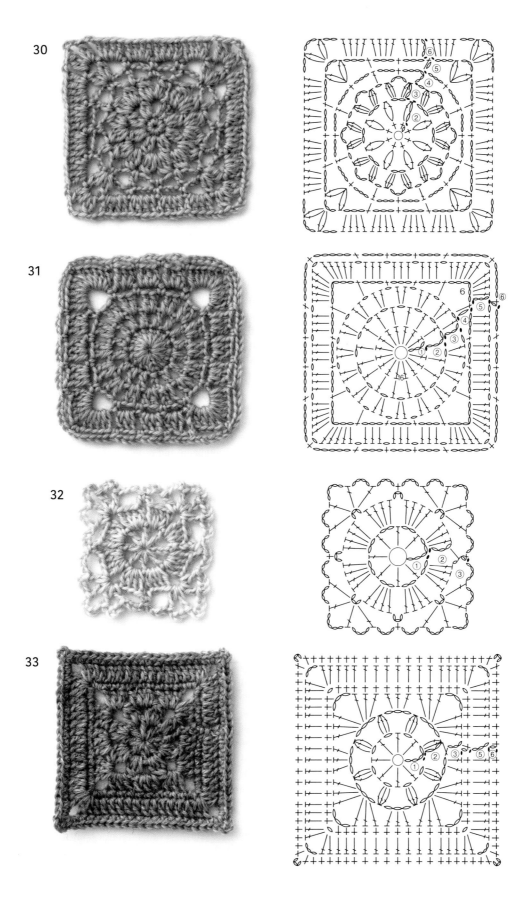

30/ Single-color or multicolor options both work well. Delicate impressions are beautiful.

31/ A stable and sturdy texture.

32/ This motif is completed in three rounds.

33/ Easy and stable crocheting with double crochet and single crochet.

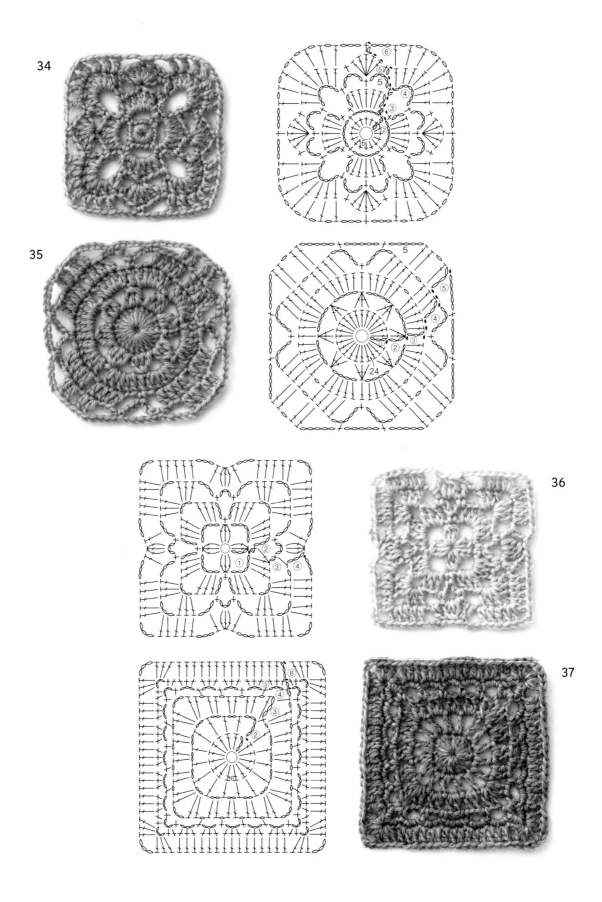

34/ The cute little square in the center.

35/ The flower in the center looks just like a sunflower.

36/ The cluster stitch accent gives a soft impression.

37/ Although it only uses double crochet, chain, and single crochet, it appears quite intricate.

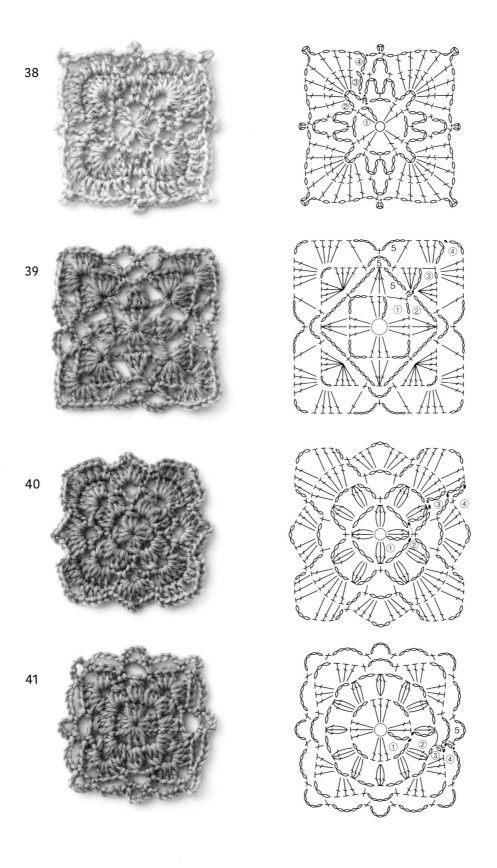

38/ Tighten the single crochets that join the chains.

39/ Gorgeous!

40/ The soft curves and sharp lines are intriguing.

41/ Connecting motifs at the center of the net results in delicate and cute pieces.

42/ How about a bolero with a fluttery and elegant motif?

44/ Small and cute!

43/ Pay attention to the high number of stitches in the center.

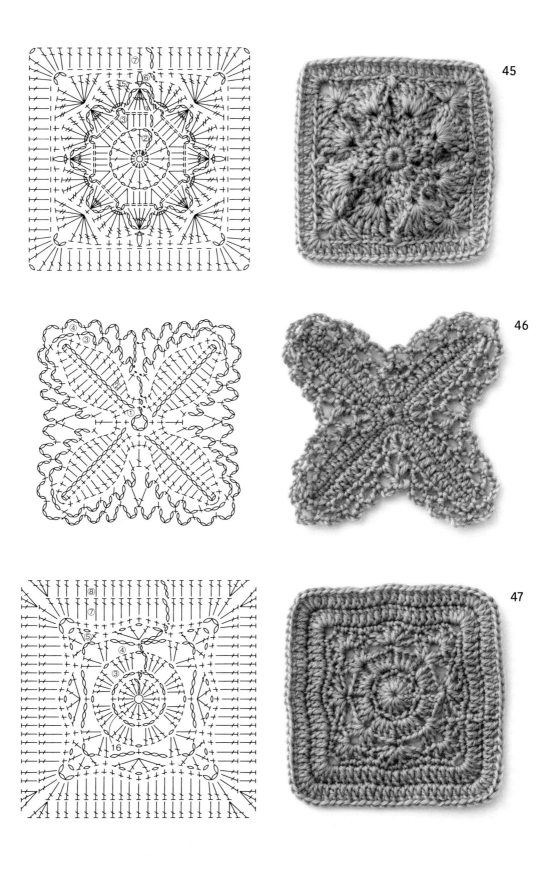

45/ Experimenting with color combinations in the round of five treble crochets yields a strong effect!

46/ The key is to make sure the lengths of the long double crochet stitches connecting the four petals are consistent.

47/ How about using colors to highlight the gentle curves?

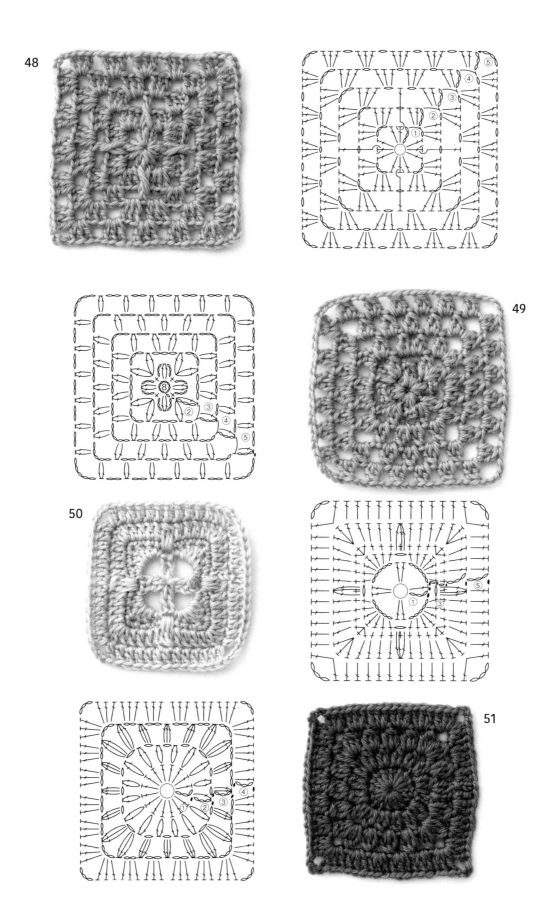

48/ The crucial point lies in firmly pulling the yarn while executing the front post double crochet.

49, 51/ Ensure the cluster stitches are of uniform size as you crochet.
50/ Try experimenting with colors.

52/ A motif that would be great for cardigans or shawls.

53/ The contrast between the small square center and the surrounding spreading petals is striking.

54/ Achieving uniformity in the height of the treble crochet is quite challenging.

Octagon, Hexagon, Triangle Motifs

Ranging from simple, repetitive designs to strikingly individualistic motifs, there's a plethora of options that will inspire you to dive in. Whether you're connecting with slip stitches, joining edges, or experimenting with rotations, embrace your creativity and let it flourish in your crafting journey!

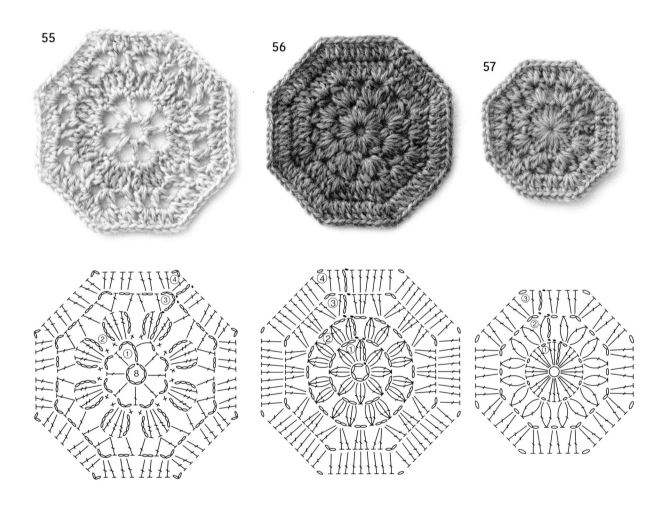

55/ When the lengths of treble stitches are aligned, the result is excellent.

56/ A pattern that is easy to understand and crochet.

57/ Crocheting with attention to the corners of the octagon.

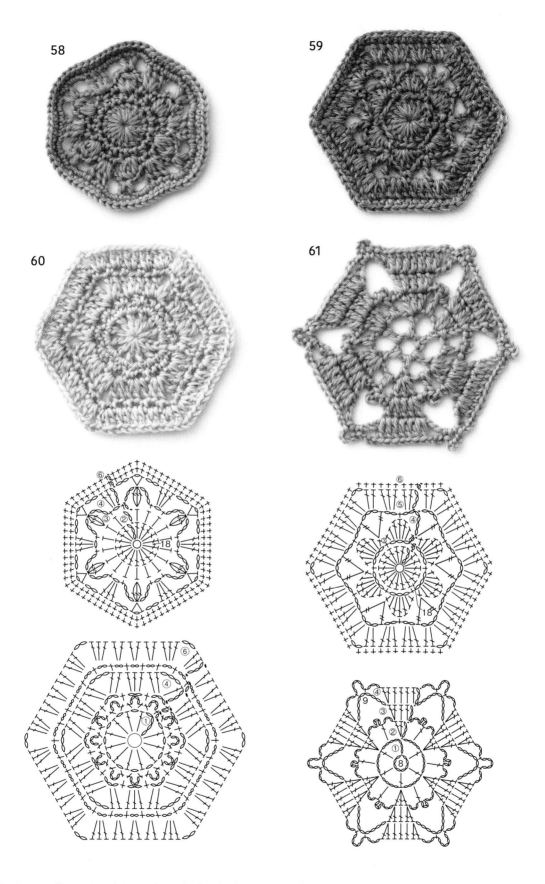

58/ Despite its small size, it achieves densely finished look with a combinations of medium-long and fine crochet stitches.

59/ The focal point is the flower shape that stands out in the center.

60/ There is an interesting change in the pattern in the second and third rounds.

61/ Because the space is large and shaping is difficult, it's helpful to visualizing the shape as you crochet.

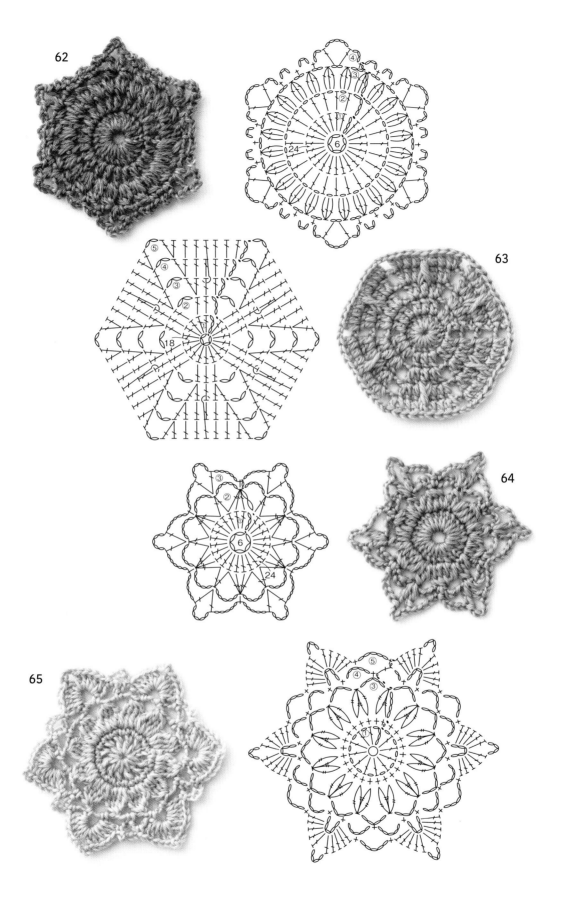

62/ It's easy to understand if you crochet the circular shape up to the third round and then connect it all at once in the fourth round.

63/ For the fifth round, make sure to pull up the front post stitches firmly and generously .

64/ A careful finish is essential for the net-based edge.

65/ The central 4-stitch treble crochet looks like flower peta

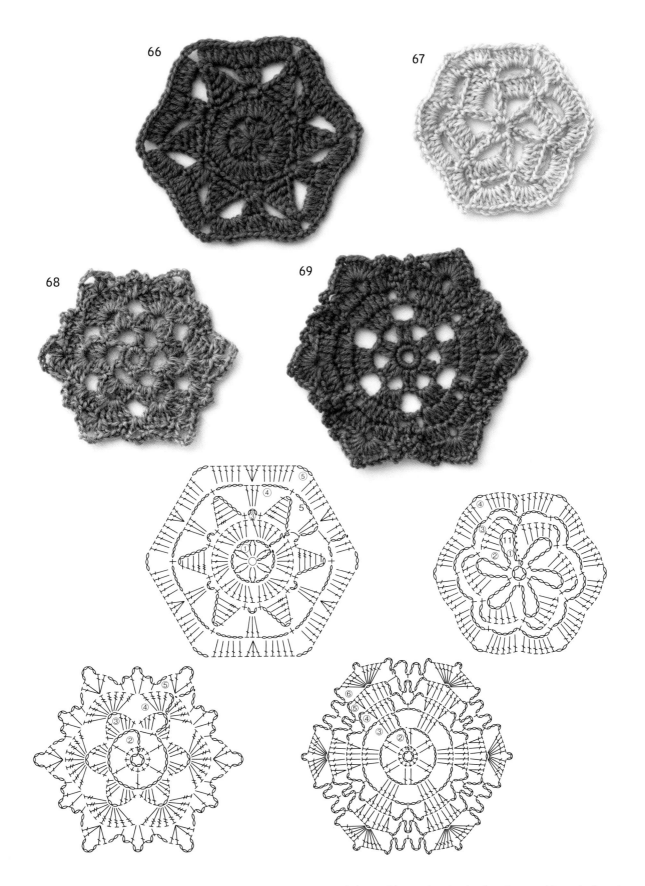

66/ The jagged triangular pattern is interesting.

67/ Does it seem like it will spin around? A pattern resembling a windmill.

68/ The treble crochet in the fourth round is a challenging point.

69/ It's challenging but rewarding. Recommended for single-use items like coasters.

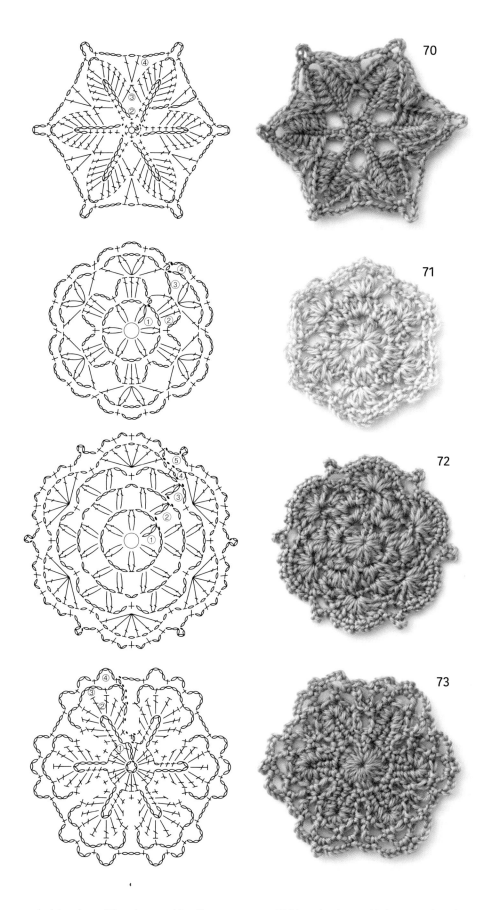

70

71

72

73

70/ Recommended to play with color combinations.

71/ Be mindful of the hexagonal shape while crocheting.

72/ Lovely shape. Make sure the picots are well-defined.

73/ A distinctive pattern. The first round, in particular, can be challenging.

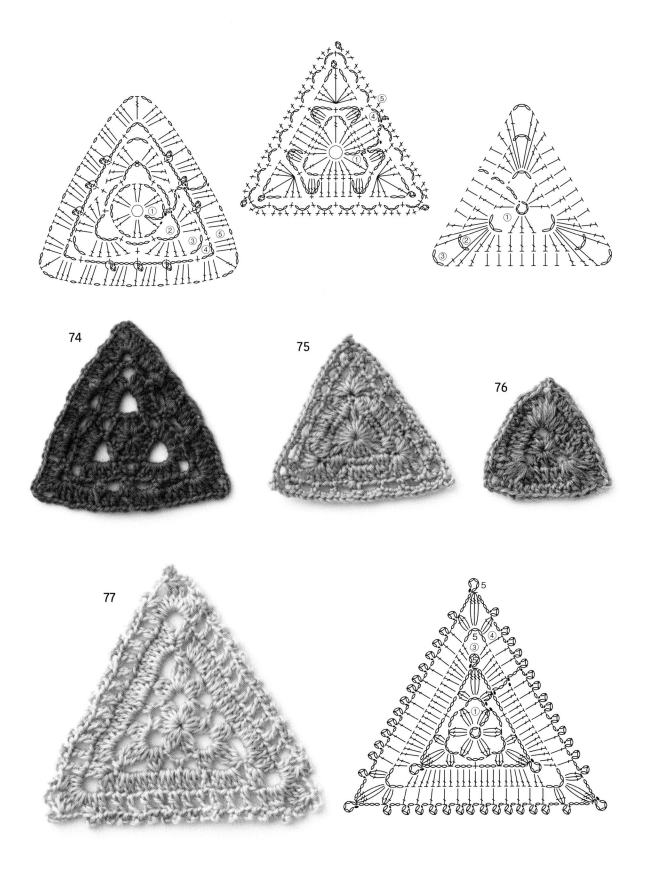

74/ It could be interesting to crochet the picot sections using various color combinations.

75/ A stable triangle. It would be interesting to try it on the jacket's border.

76/ Using double crochet at the corners creates a slightly rounded triangular shape, making color usage particularly effective.

77/ Crocheting the double crochet evenly at the same height results in a beautiful finish.

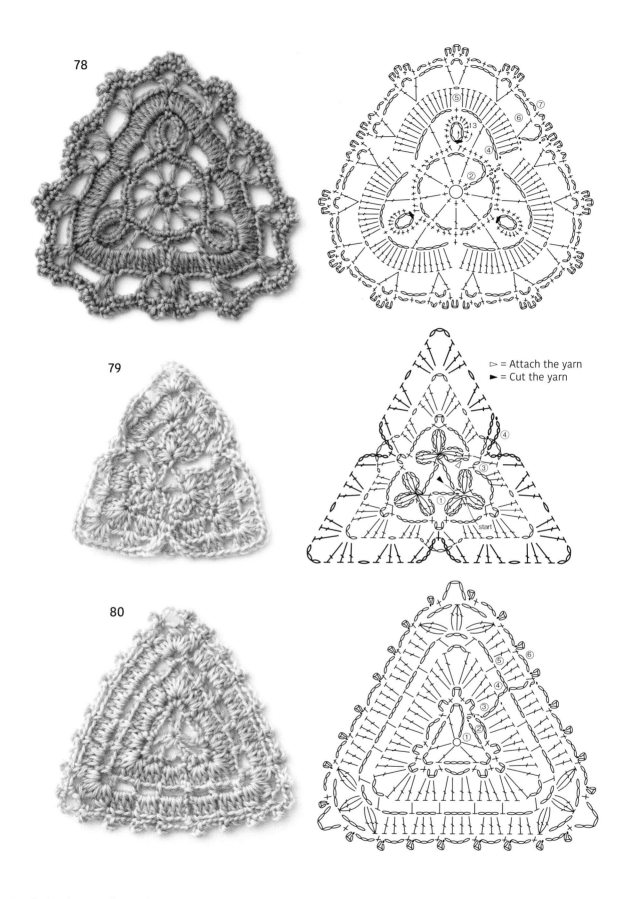

78 A distinctive motif. Join them into a shawl or use one piece as on accent, like a patch.

79 A motif featuring a small flower hidden in the center, resembling three small triangles fused together.

80 Ideal for joining into garments or for use as border accents.

▷ = Attach the yarn
► = Cut the yarn

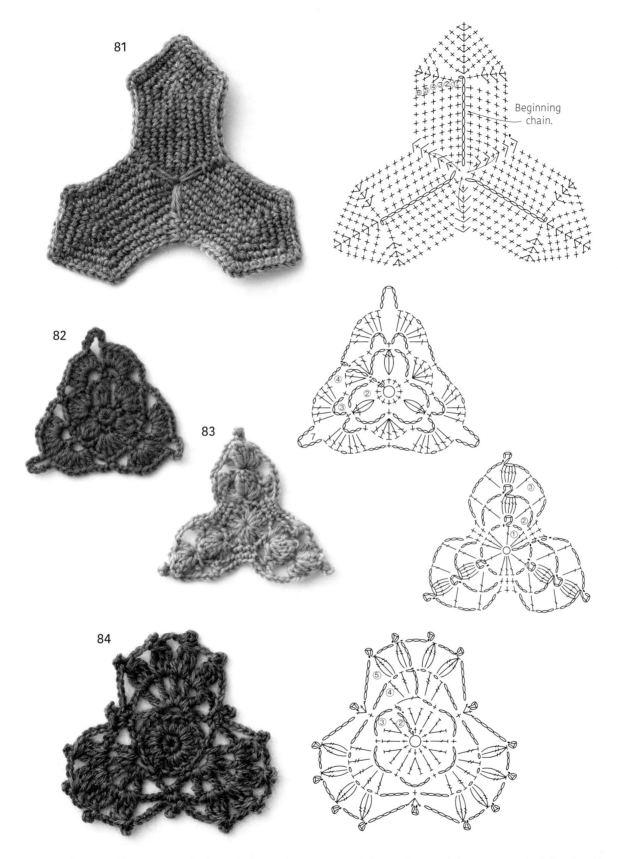

81 Beginning chain.

82

83

84

81/ A motif irresistible to those who love single crochet, though care must be taken as the number of rounds on the left and right sides may vary due to the chain being in the center.

82/ A motif that you'd want to connect into trapezoids, hexagons, and various other shapes, offering a wide range of applications.

83/ The puffiness of the popcorn stitch is adorable! Combining small motifs can lead to intriguing designs.

84/ Depending on how they're connected, various styles can be explored. It's fun to experiment with making wearables.

= Y-shaped stitch

85

86

87

85/ Beautiful curved pattern reminiscent of plants. It's easier to crochet than it looks.

86/ Pay attention to the balance of the chains while crocheting for a neat result.

87/ Finish the edges with mesh crochet, and it looks cute as it is.

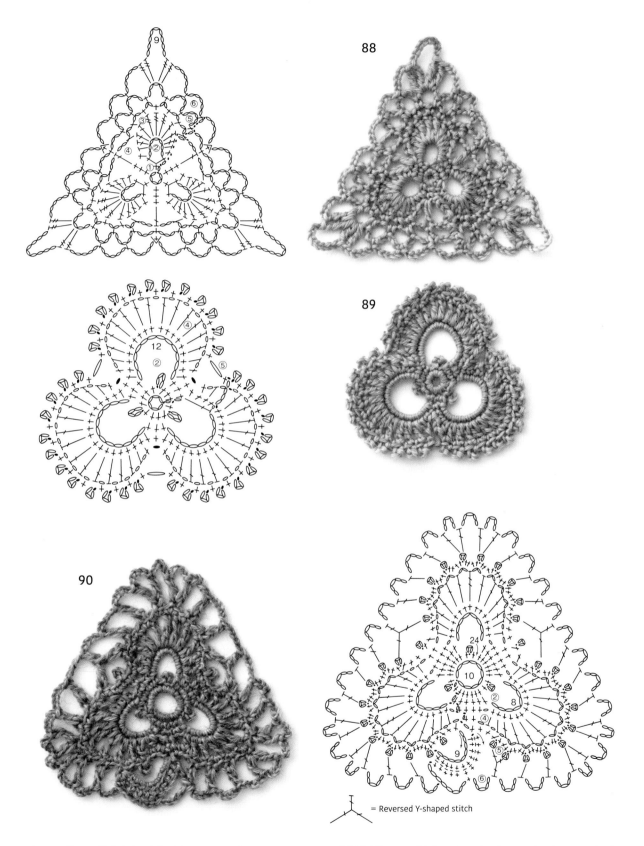

88

89

90

= Reversed Y-shaped stitch

88/ Even if you finish it with thinner yarn for a more delicate look, it will still be lovely.

89/ Using the large round hole as a buttonhole is also interesting!

90/ Adding multiple colors to the center has sparked an interest in crocheting a shawl.

Circular Motifs

At first glance, circular motifs may seem complex, but with a keen eye for pattern repetition, they can be crocheted easily. Small circles give a delicate impression, while larger ones exude elegance! Experimenting with different materials and colors can help you find the motif that suits you best.

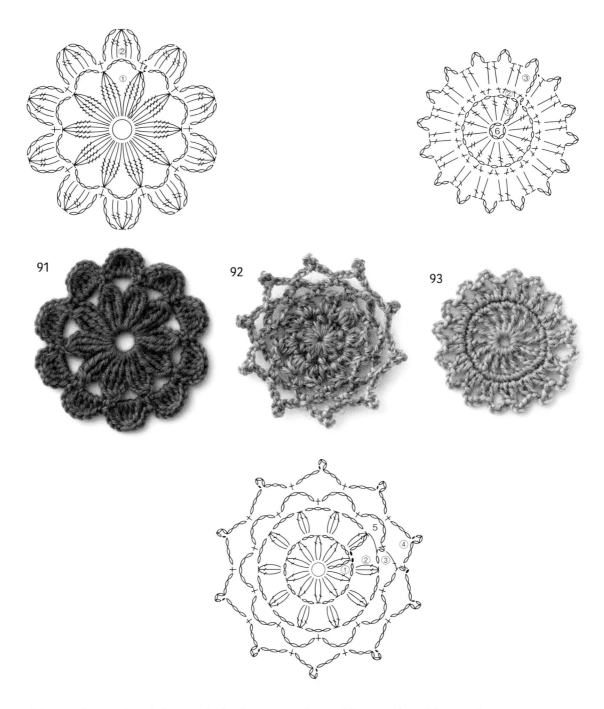

91/ Be careful not to loosen the stitches on the hook when working with quadruple-wrapped long stitches. It can be used as a brooch on its own, or you could try joining them together for a waistcoat.

92/ A sparkling motif reminiscent of a star.

93/ A versatile motif that could be used for anything.

94/ The lines of single crochet create a beautiful loop. By joining them, you can create squares, triangles, circles, and many possibilities.

95/ Like flowers blooming towards the sky. Seems perfect for a scarf.

96/ By linking octagons in a ring, it gives off a soft ambiance, ideal for designs like daisies.

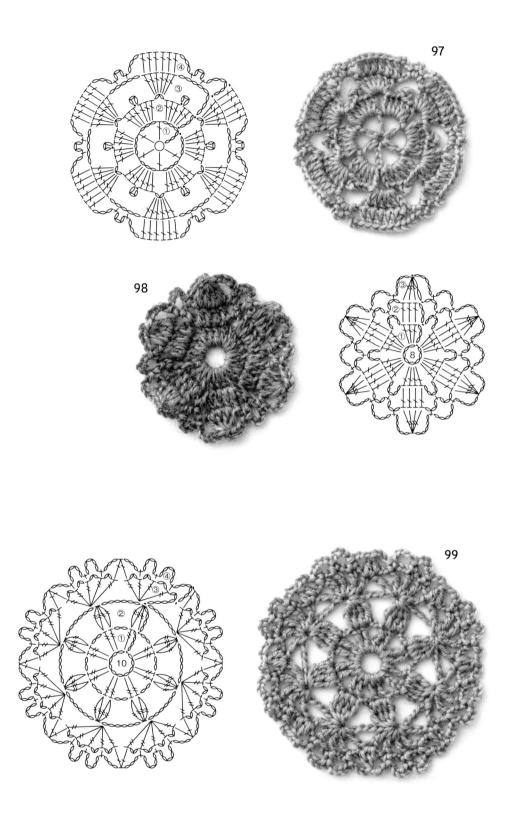

97

98

99

97/ With a balanced and clean shape, it seems to suit anything.

98/ Weather in one color or a mix, this easy-to-make cute motif would look great in a bolero.

99/ This gorgeous motif, with its translucent quality, is ideal for compact wearables such as French sleeve tops or vests.

100/ Since the outer part is made with net stitch, it highlights the center and makes for a light piece.

101/ Resembling rose petals. How about connecting them in a row for a tie or a belt?

102/ This charming motif, with a star-like center, would look great on a scarf or other garments.

103/ The combination of double crochet and net stitch creates a beautiful line when joined.

104,105/ It resembles a sparkler, with a crackling effect. Suitable for shawls and similar items.

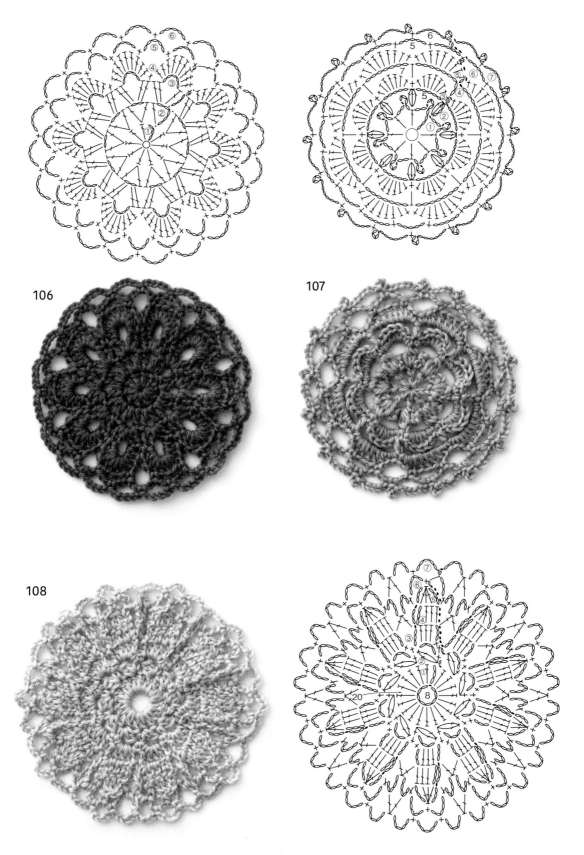

106

107

108

106/ Resembling a chrysanthemum flower, you need to adjust tension while the hook working the 9 double crochet petal stitches. Ideal for crafting a French sleeve pullover.

107/ The central cluster stitches and picot edges add a touch of elegance to this motif.

108/ It's recommended to crochet with multiple colors rather than a single color for this motif, which is more suitable for advanced crafters due to its slightly higher difficulty level.

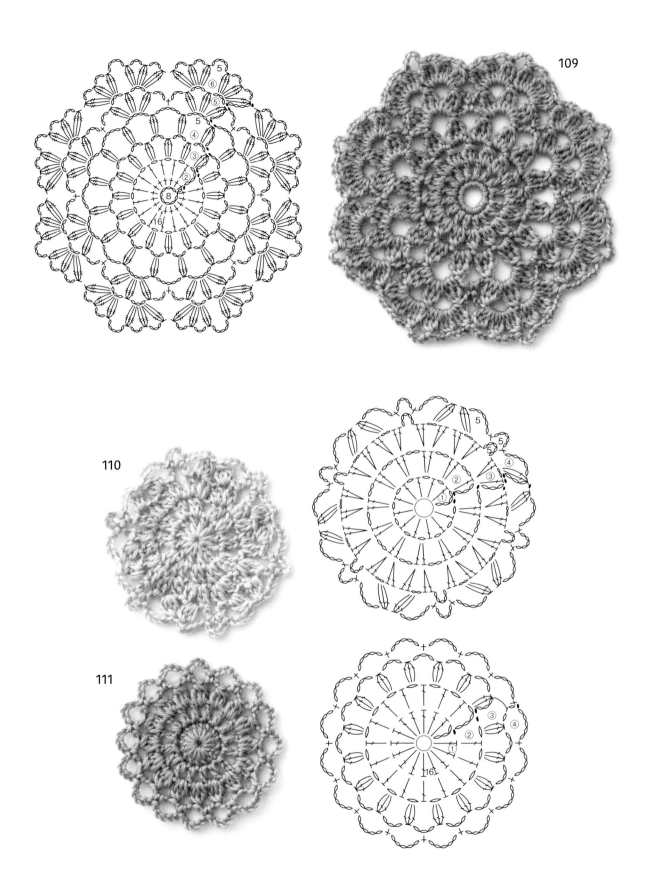

109/ With an impression reminiscent of a lotus flower, this motif is ideal for crafting both loose-fitting garments and sleeves.

110/ A motif that is both sheer and sturdy in its crochet fabric.

111/ The beautiful circle resembles a dahlia flower, perfect for incorporating into boleros or cardigans.

112/ Like sunflowers blooming towards the sun, this motif is large and easy to crochet, making it perfect for creating oversized shawls.

113/ This motif features a delicate transparency, making

it easy to crochet. It's ideal for crafting lightweight triangular shawls.

114/ Reminiscent of intricate geometric designs, it sparks curiosity, offering a sense of wonder upon closer inspection.

115/ The sharp-edged border gives it a distinctive look. The cluster stitch of six stitches in the third round poses a challenge.

116/ Surrounded by four-leaf clovers, this motif looks suitable for shawls.

117/ The pointed ends of the picots add a light and lively touch.

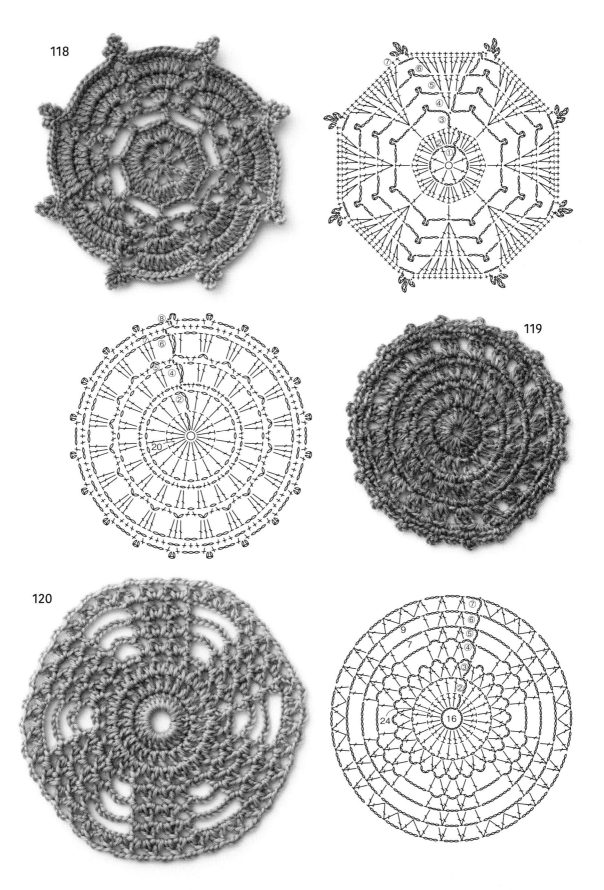

118/ The triple picots along the edge add a playful touch.

119/ A motif with a pattern resembling tree rings. It would be interesting to arrange it in large, medium, and small motifs.

120/ For the seventh round of double crochet stitches, it's important to determine whether to split the previous round to crochet or to crochet around a bundle.

Flower-Like Motifs

With shapes reminiscent of flower petals, these eye-catching motifs can be used alone to add flair to simple accessories or as decorative edges on clothing. They are also great for assembling into collars or shawls.

※ In the 4th round, work single crochet by inserting the hook between the stitches of the previous round.

121

122

123

124

121/ An adaptable motif that looks highly practical.

122/ Looks fun when joined with multiple colors.

123/ A cute flower motif that stands out on its own. Perfect for shawls and garments.

124/ A tiny motif that inspires you to keep joining more.

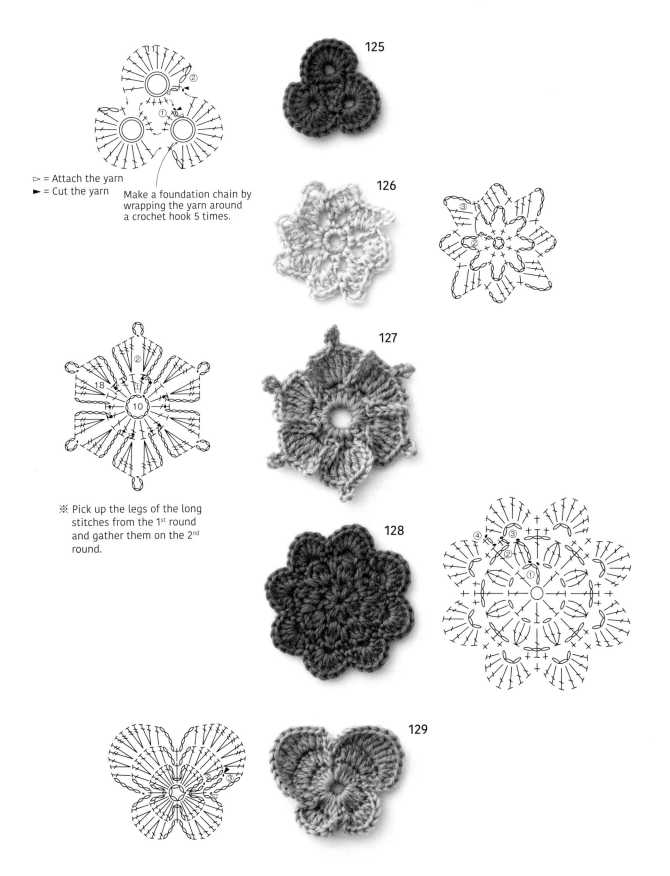

▷ = Attach the yarn

► = Cut the yarn

Make a foundation chain by wrapping the yarn around a crochet hook 5 times.

125

126

127

128

129

※ Pick up the legs of the long stitches from the 1ˢᵗ round and gather them on the 2ⁿᵈ round.

125/ You can make a foundation chain to crochet, but making magic ring is recommended.

126/ Pay attention to the number of chains in the third round.

127/ You can change the colors of the flower center (first round) and petals (second round).

128/ The finished piece has a solid thickness to it. While solid colors are charming, using multiple colors adds an interesting touch.

129/ It brings to mind pansies or butterflies. Would you like to use it as a focal point?

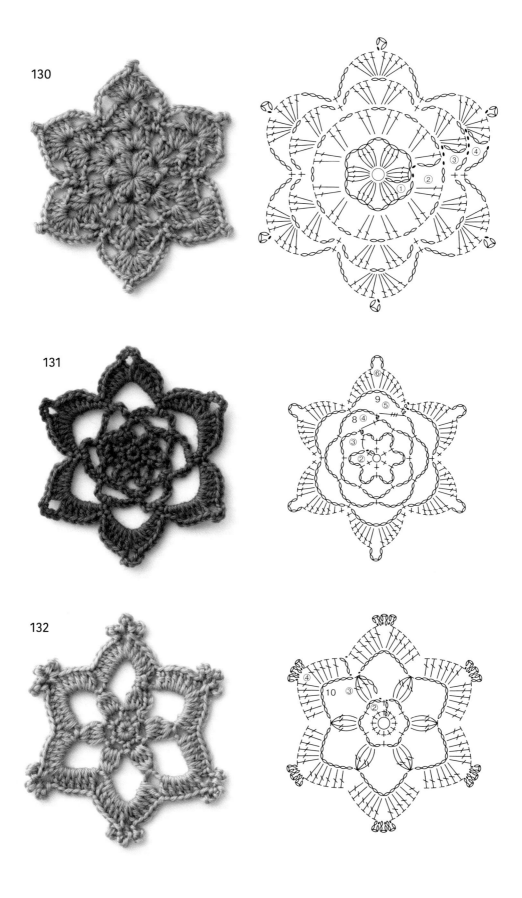

130/ The popcorn stitch in the center looks cute.

131/ Considering the motif's ease of crocheting, attempting a large shawl or something similar seems enticing.

132/ Simple yet gives off a lively impression.

133

134

135

133/ A standout piece that makes you want to take a second look.

134/ A flat flower motif that would suit scarves and shawls.

135/ With a large number of stitches, it's a motif you'd want to crochet carefully and take your time with. The sense of accomplishment upon completion is significant.

136

🪝 = In the 4th round, work the double crochet bobble stitches by inserting the hook into the slip picot.

137

138

Note: In 3rd round, work single crochets by picking up the loops between the stitches of the previous round.

136/ This motif looks like a throwing star. Ensure proper balance to prevent it from curling.

137/ A gorgeous shaped motif with a distinctive design.

138/ Lots of double crochets make this motif easy and stable to crochet.

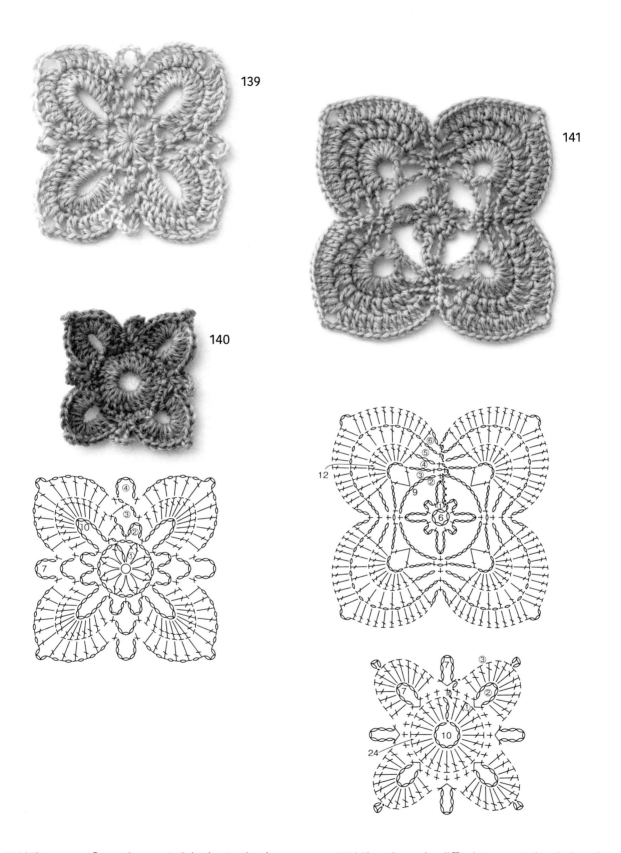

139/ The square flower is easy to join due to the dense double crochet stitches.

140/ Despite its small size, this motif stands out. The combination of double crochets and spaces is perfectly balanced.

141/ Since it can be difficult to count the chains where you work two double crochets in the third round, it's helpful to place markers on those chains.

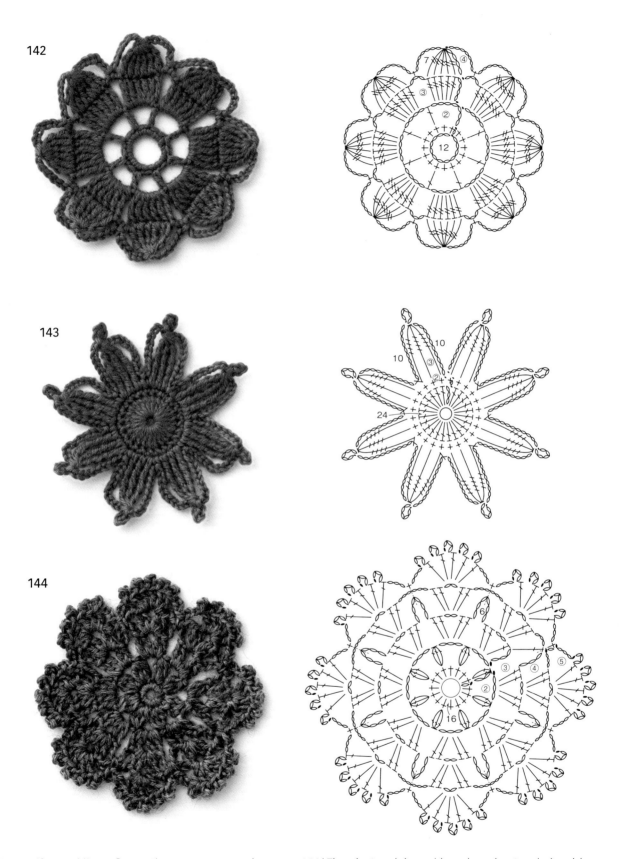

142/ A motif resembling a flower. The generous central opening lends it a lightness.

143/ The quadruple treble crochets in the petals can be quite challenging.

144/ The picots edging adds a charming touch, inspiring to crochet quadruple a shawl .

145/ A cute motif that mixes stars and flowers, perfect for adding accents to garments or accessories.

146/ Easy to crochet, making it suitable for beginners.

147/ A three-dimensional petal motif. You would like to try crocheting it in various colors.

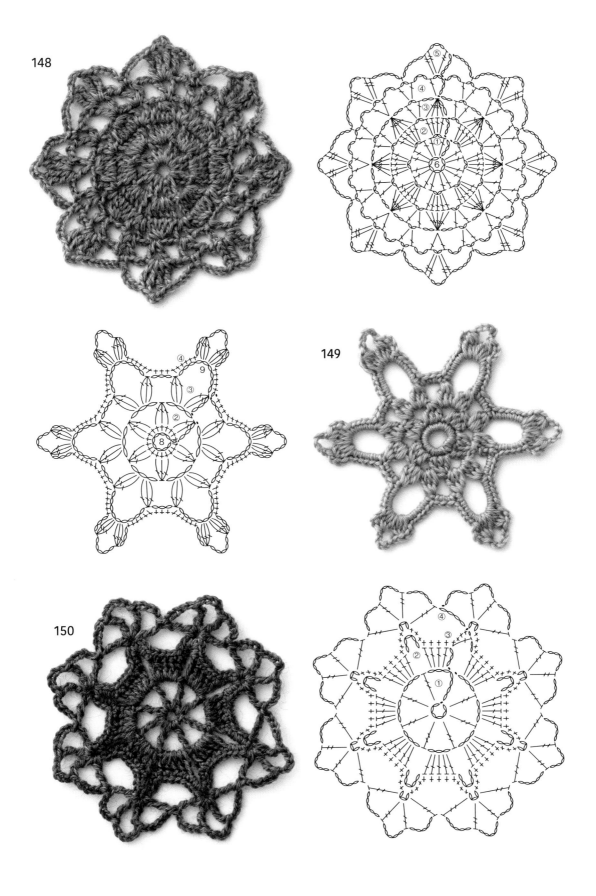

148

149

150

148/ The balance between stitches and transparency is good, making it easy to crochet.

149/ This motif, with its single-line drawing-like lines, requires attention to prevent any misshaping.

150/ It seems interesting to join them together and create a finished piece.

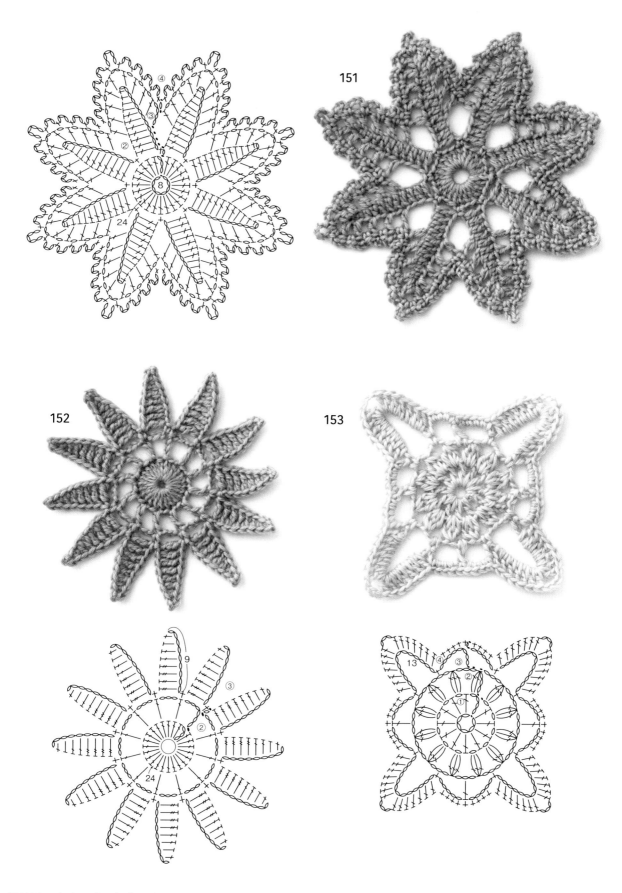

151/ It's admittedly challenging to crochet because it's quite frilly, but the resulting elegance is very appealing.

152/ The final zigzag edge tends to curl, so finishing is crucial!

153/ Bold motifs with large holes require careful attention to prevent distortion.

176

177

178

179

※ For the popcorn stitches in the third round of double crochet, insert the hook as if you're catching a slip stitch picot.

176/ It might be interesting to combine it with knitting projects!

177/ A cute motif reminiscent of small flowers.

178/ It might be interesting to crochet in different color combination.

179/ The popcorn stitches falling sideways all around are quite distinctive.

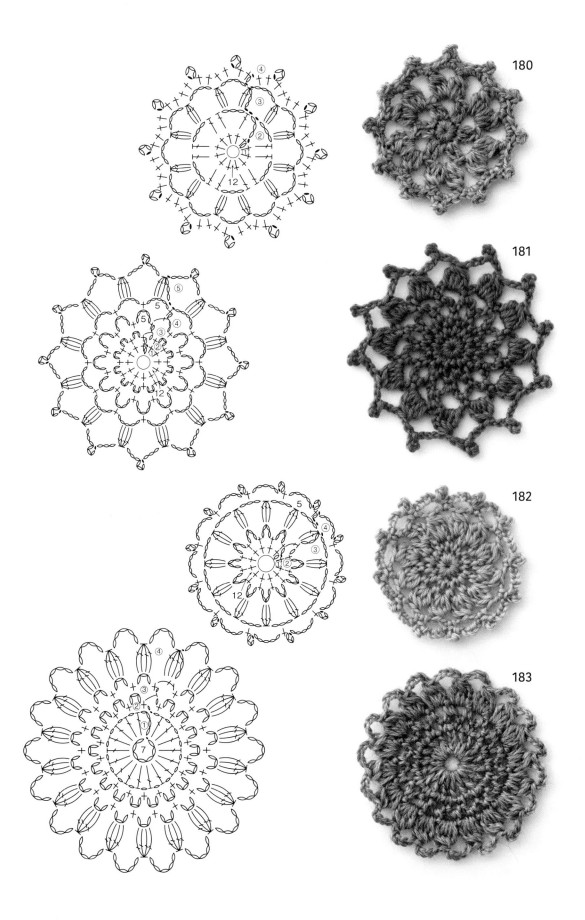

180

181

182

183

180/ Ideal for adding accents to collars and hems.

181,183/ The pattern repetition is simple and easy to crochet.

182/ Even though it's small, the motif stands out.

184

185

186

※ For the 3rd round, work single crochets by inserting the hook between the stitches of the previous round.

184/ Puff stitch made with treble crochet is impressive!

185/ Crochet with various colors and materials, then join them for blankets, bags, and more.

186/ The central flower pattern would look great crocheted in a variety of colors.

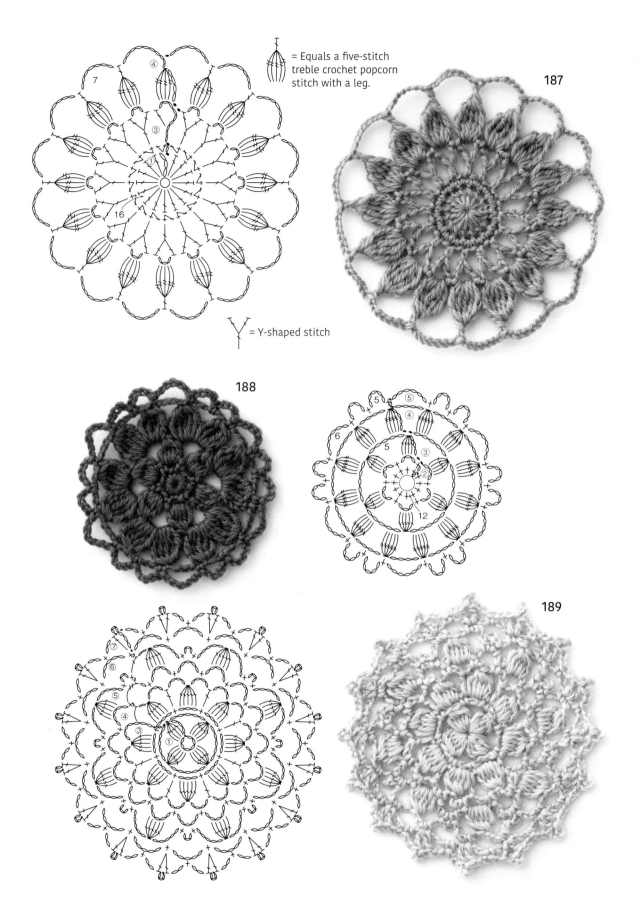

= Equals a five-stitch treble crochet popcorn stitch with a leg.

Y = Y-shaped stitch

187

188

189

187/ The third round consists of "Y-shaped stitches", and the fourth round consists of "five stitch treble crochet stitch with leg". A bit challenging!

188/ The shape and stitches of the motif are round and cute.

189/ A single motif with 20 popcorn stitches! Aim to become a popcorn stitch expert.

190,191/ Puffy half-double crochet bobbles are charming.

192/ For the double crochet in the third round, insert into the bobble stitch of the first round, folding the stitches of the second round forward.

193/ It might be easy to make a mistake at the point where 3 single crochets are worked into 1 chain stitch in the sixth round.

194/ Full and fluffy "7 double crochet popcorn stitch".

195/ Highlight the zigzag lines around the edge for a sharp finish.

196/ A stunning total of 42 popcorn stitches! Ideal for making cushions or mats with thick yarn.

197/ Join many of them and make wearable items.

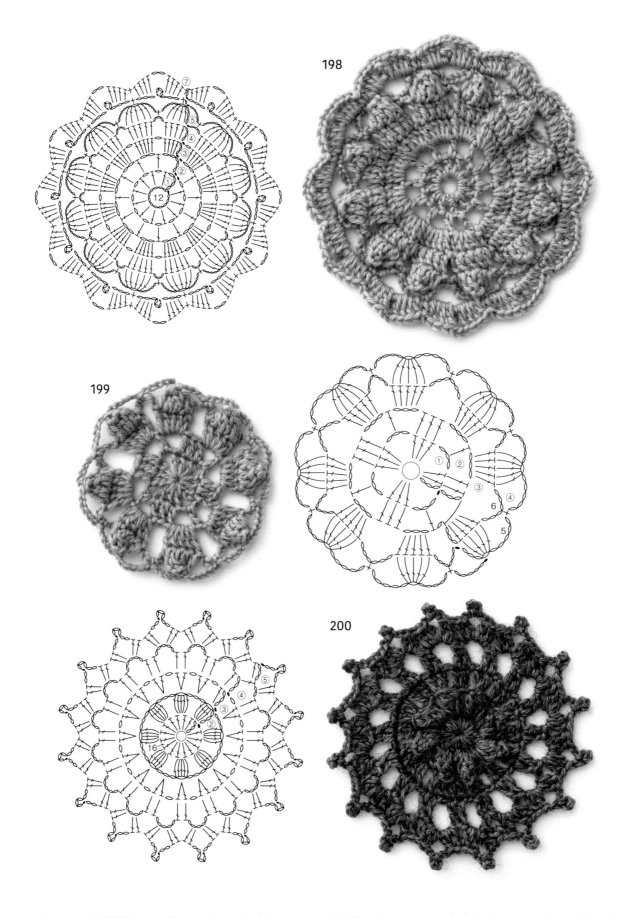

198/ A large and fullfilling motif to crochet. Ideal for shawls or wraps.

199/ Do you see the pattern around the motifs resembling cupcakes?

200/ For the popcorn stitch in the second round, insert the hook between the double crochet stitches of the first round.

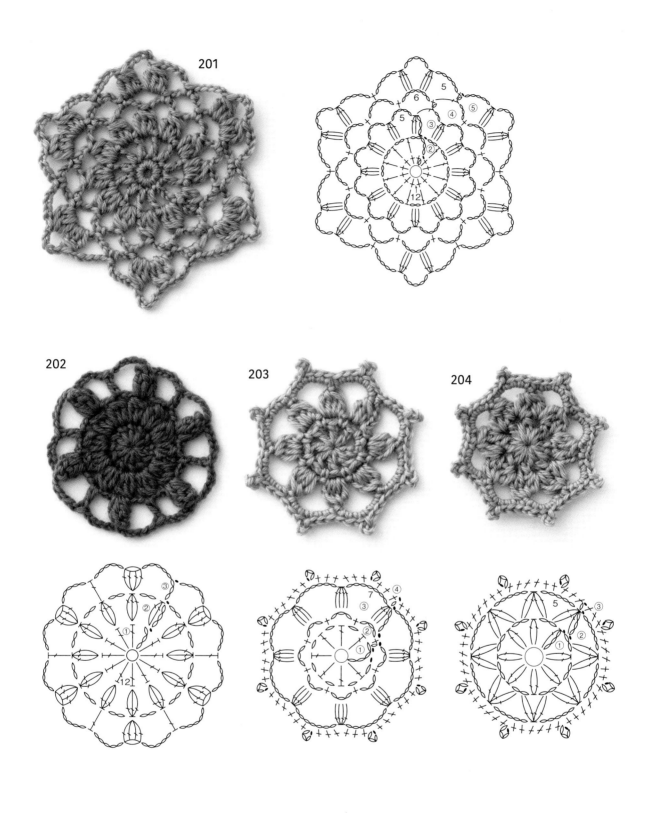

201/ Easy to crochet and versatile for any project.
202/ The four-stitch popcorn stitch adds a striking touch.

203,204/ Using single crochet stitches around the edge adds stability. Color coordination is also recommended.

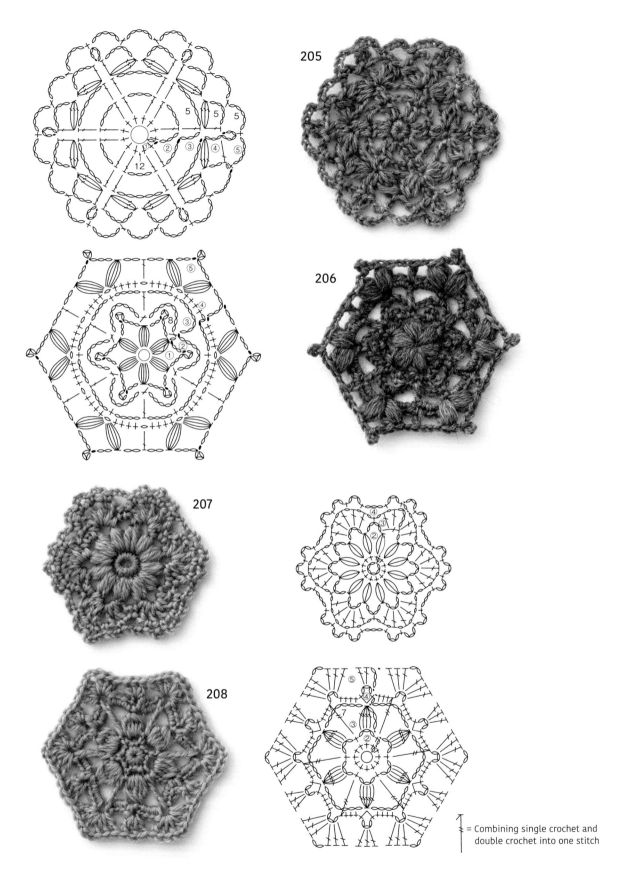

205

206

207

208

5 5 5

12

8

₤ = Combining single crochet and
double crochet into one stitch

205/ The key point is the bobble stitches aligned
diagonally, looking like they are head-to-head.

206,207/ The key to successfully crocheting half double
crochet bobble stitches is to maintain uniform size and
height.

208/ By using different colors for just the bobble stitch
round, the bobbles appear to stand out and look adorable.

= Popcorn stitch with a foundation of 3 double crochet stitches

209/ The key feature is the 'popcorn stitch with a base of 3 double crochet stitches' in the petals.

210/ The picots around the edge following the popcorn stitches add a touch of elegance.

211/ Medium-length popcorn stitches are always crocheted with consistent tension to achieve a plump appearance.

212/ An easy-to-crochet and cute pattern that highlights the beauty of popcorn stitches.

213 / Eye-catching! A single piece used as an appliqué adds a stylish touch.

214 / 24 popcorn stitches line up in one round. It could be interesting to use it partially, such as on the hem of a garment.

215 / A motif that looks like small flowers joined together. The key is to keep the size of the popcorn stitches consistent.

216/ A striking popcorn stitch flower based on treble crochet.

217/ It's cute to make a bug in bright colors or connect them in a braid.

218/ Achieving the right balance of stitches in the second round, "long crochet to quadruple crochet", can be challenging.

Dimensional Crochet Motifs

These motifs showcase the distinctiveness of crochet by layering stitches to form petals and ruffles, incorporating previous round stitches, and using raised stitches for volume. The impact of these motifs is heightened with effective color use.

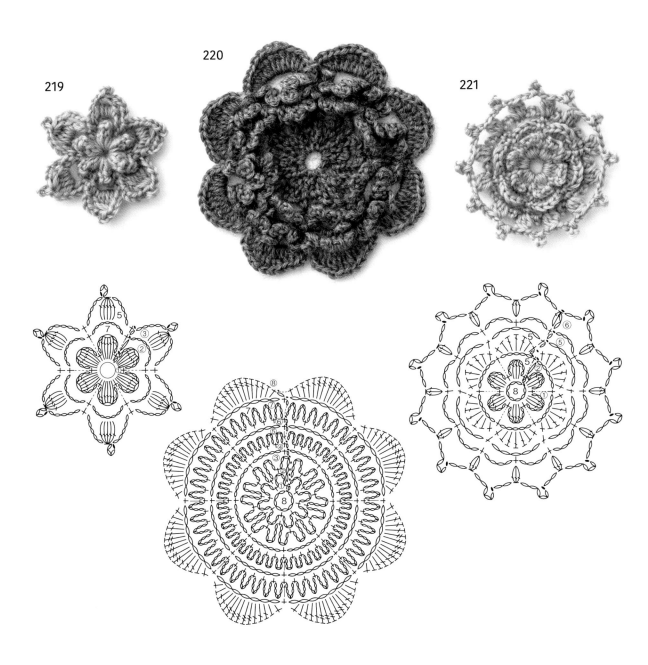

219/ In this small motif, the central popcorn stitch becomes the focal point.

220/ Finish carefully to ensure the frills are not flattened.

221/ The picots around the edge are cute.

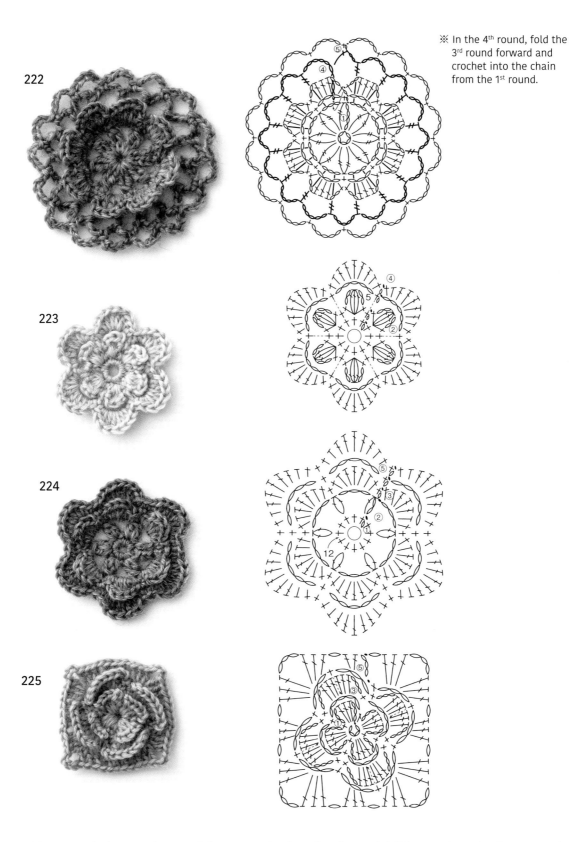

222

223

224

225

※ In the 4th round, fold the 3rd round forward and crochet into the chain from the 1st round.

222/ The contrast between the lacy net base and the three-dimensional petals is enjoyable.

223,224/ Pay attention to creating clean curves when crocheting the petals.

225/ Overlapping and shifting petals evoke the image of a rose flower.

226/ Make sure the two layers of petals are offset from each other as you crochet.

227/ It seems easy to join with netting around the edge.

228/ Pay attention to the height of stitches to ensure smooth curves for the petals.

※ In 4th round, tilt the stitches from the previous round forward and crochet into the chain from 2nd round.

Note: In 6th round, wrap the double crochet stitches around the previous round and crochet into the single crochet from 4th round.

※ For the back post single crochet in the 3rd and 5th rounds, crochet around the stitches of the 1st and 3rd rounds.

229

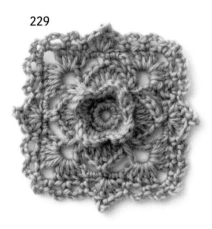

230

231

229/ It looks like you can join the pieces freely with some creative thinking.

230/ It would be fun to choose a color scheme that resembles flowers and leaves.

231/ A bold design with a circular shape, bobble stitch, and raised flowers.

Picot

Tilt the picot forward and crochet into the bundle as if following an arrow.

232

233

234

235

232/ Pay attention to the stability of the net pattern in the first round.

233/ A very basic flower motif.

234, 235/ Despite its small size, it's a square motif with a strong presence.

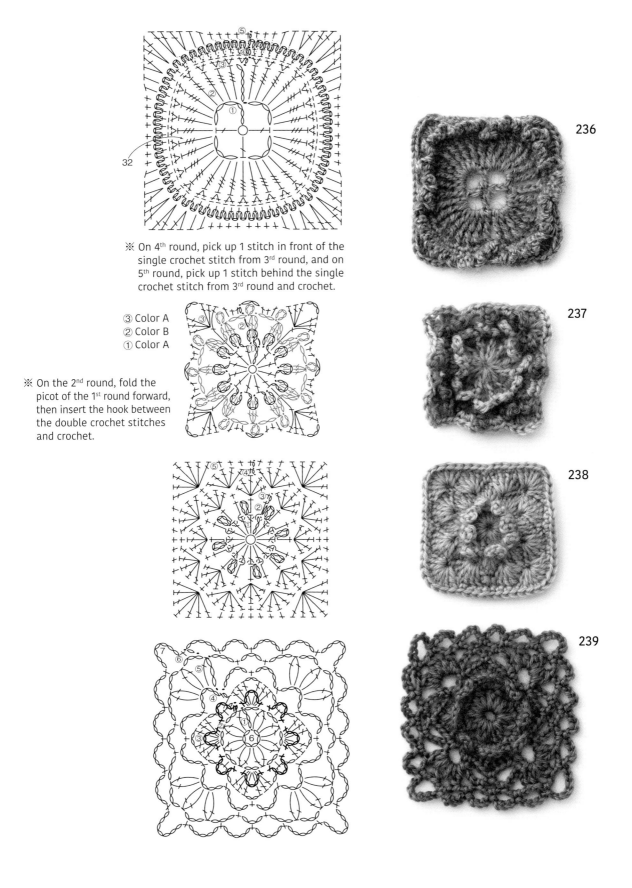

※ On 4th round, pick up 1 stitch in front of the single crochet stitch from 3rd round, and on 5th round, pick up 1 stitch behind the single crochet stitch from 3rd round and crochet.

③ Color A
② Color B
① Color A

※ On the 2nd round, fold the picot of the 1st round forward, then insert the hook between the double crochet stitches and crochet.

236

237

238

239

236/ Picking up half stitches in fourth and fifth rounds is somewhat more challenging.

237/ The corners in the third round are an adaptation of the Y-stitch.

238/ A pattern resembling densely packed shells. It's interesting how the image changes when different colors are used.

239/ Ensure that the central petal-shaped net pattern remains neat and does not get misshaped.

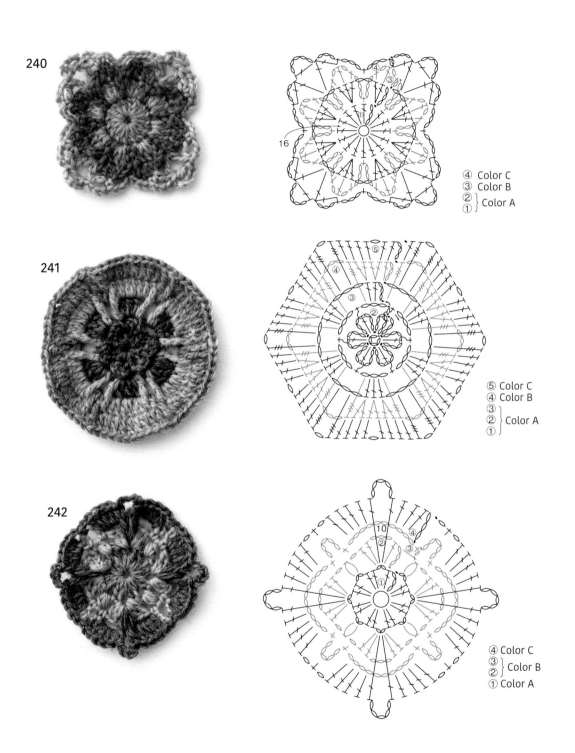

240

④ Color C
③ Color B
②
① } Color A

241

⑤ Color C
④ Color B
③
②
① } Color A

242

④ Color C
③
② } Color B
① Color A

16

10

240/ When you incorporate colors in your crochet, the flower patterns will become more visible.

241/ In second round, turn the motif to the wrong side and crochet.

242/ When the motifs are joined, the way the corner lines appear looks intriguing.

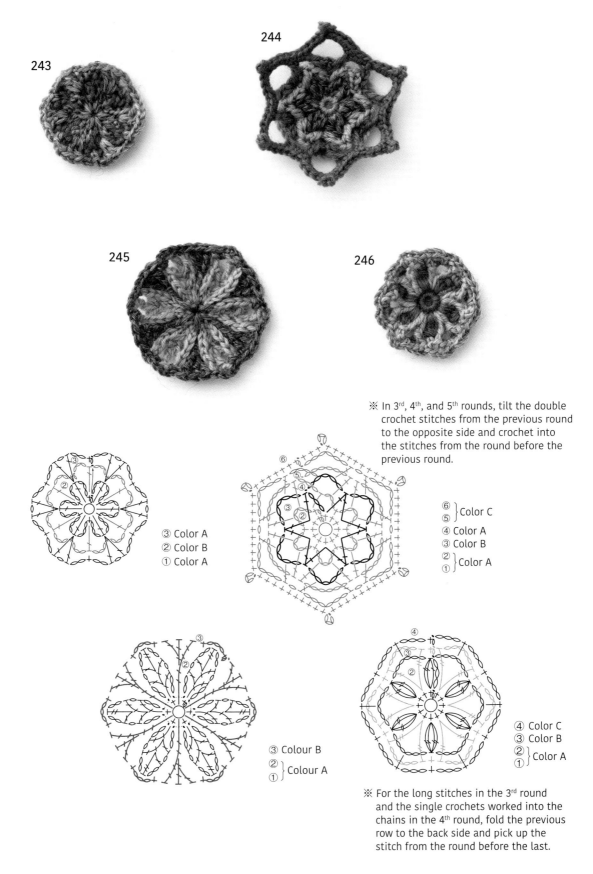

243

244

245

246

※ In 3rd, 4th, and 5th rounds, tilt the double crochet stitches from the previous round to the opposite side and crochet into the stitches from the round before the previous round.

③ Color A
② Color B
① Color A

⑥
⑤ } Color C
④ Color A
③ Color B
②
① } Color A

③ Colour B
②
① } Colour A

④ Color C
③ Color B
②
① } Color A

※ For the long stitches in the 3rd round and the single crochets worked into the chains in the 4th round, fold the previous row to the back side and pick up the stitch from the round before the last.

243/ The small motifs feature striking circular petals.

244,246/ Pay attention to the flow of the pattern and be mindful of the stitches' orientation.

245/ The intricate stitches resembling leaf veins in the second round are a combination of Y-stitches. Mastering them will level up your skills.

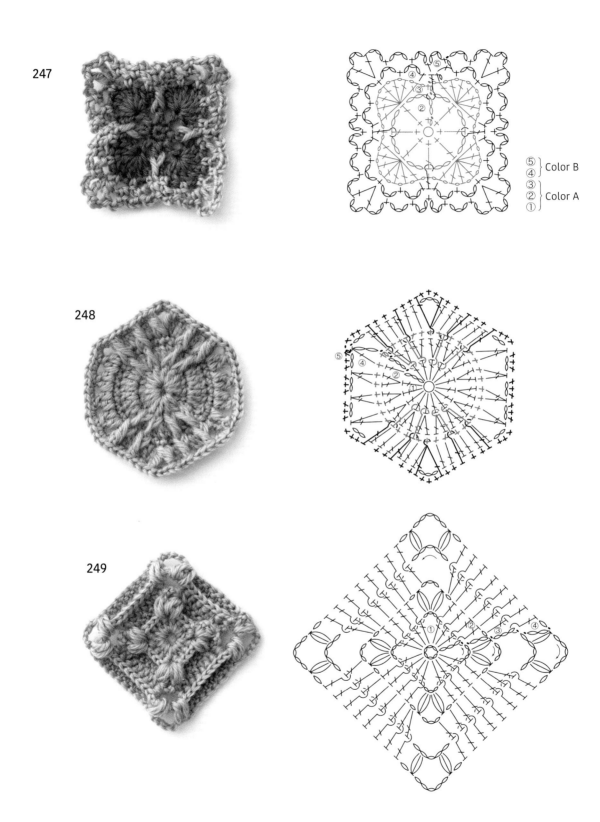

247

248

249

⑤ } Color B
④
③ } Color A
②
①

247/ In fourth round, the raised stitches are created by pulling the yarn out sharply.

248,249/ The raised stitch lines are impactful, and connecting them is expected to create interesting effects.

250/ The circular petals are striking. Easy to connect together with mesh stitch.

251/ The motif has a special shape—does it resemble a pansy?

252/ The mysterious undulation of the crochet fabric. You can expand the crochet as much as you like.

Lacy Motifs

Featuring a beautiful contrast between the stitches and their transparency, this lacy motif is made with cotton lace yarn. This type of yarn slides easily compared to wool and can lead to loose stitches, so it's important to manage your yarn tension and tighten the stitches as you work.

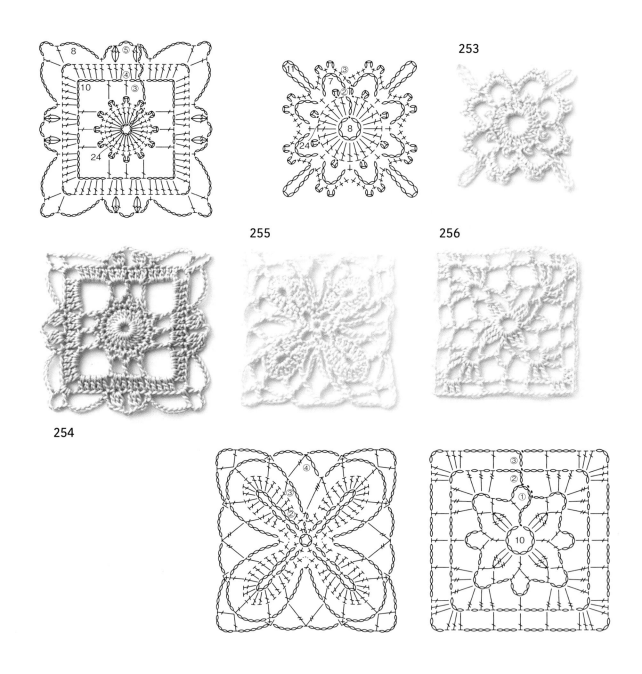

253/ Use the loops in the four corners to join the pieces together.

254/ Double crochets worked into the center provide stability and ease of crochet.

255/ A pattern resembling a four-leaf clover.

256/ The bobble stitch version features a crossed double crochet stitch with four wraps of yarn. It seems like the first round could be challenging.

257

258

259

257, 258/ When joining the motifs, the corner patterns align to form lines, creating an entirely new motif.

259/ The net pattern, resembling frills, looks luxurious.

260 / The cute flower in the center is lovely.

261 / Motifs that you'd like to use for shawls or skirts.

262 / A crochet pattern inspired by a sunflower.

263/ A motif featuring a delicate pineapple pattern.
264/ Pay attention to the balance between triple treble crochet and chain stitches.

265/ In the fifth round, there's a part where the stitching direction reverses, so be careful not to get lost.

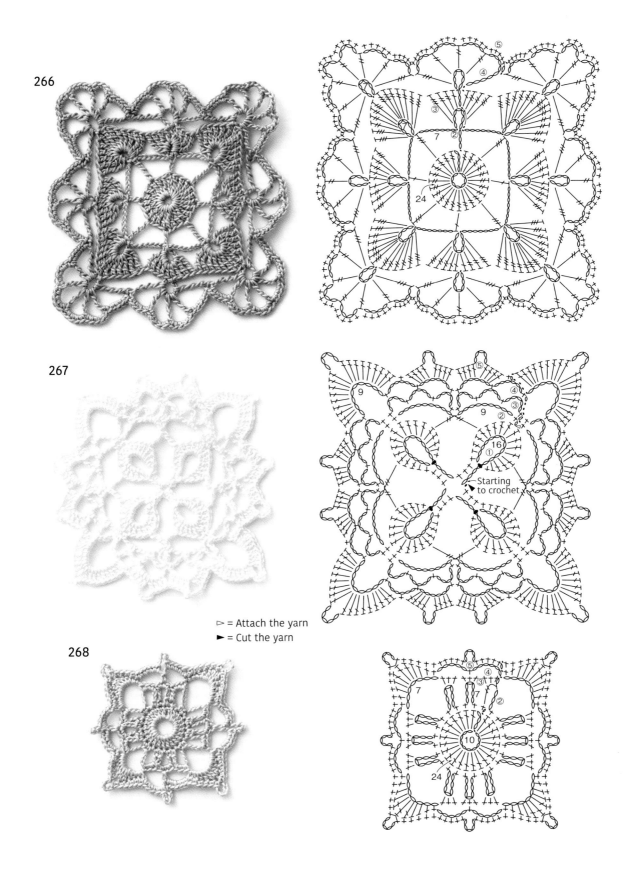

266

267

▷ = Attach the yarn
► = Cut the yarn

268

266/ As you can see, this motif offers a satisfying challenge.

267/ A crest-like pattern. After finishing the first round, cut the yarn and start the second round with a new strand.

268/ It's circular until the second round, then becomes square from the third round onwards.

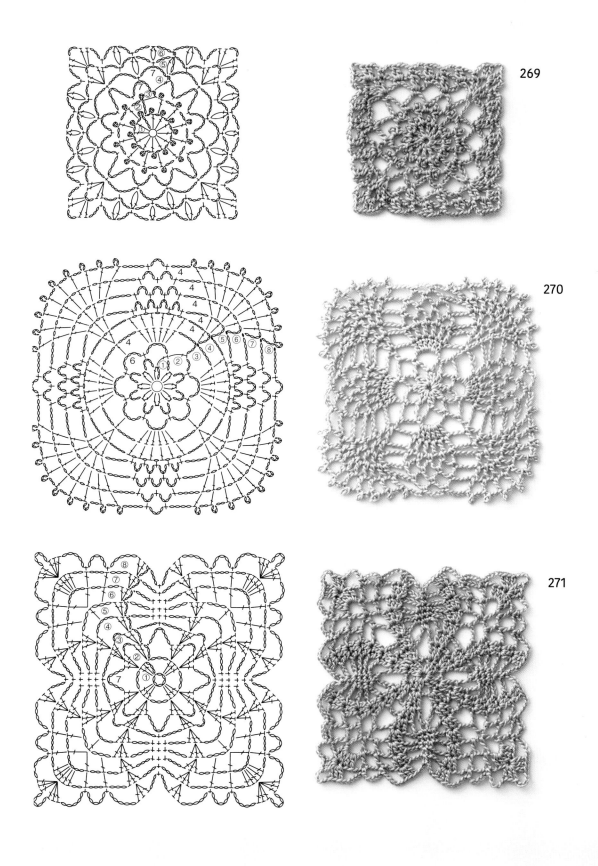

269

270

271

269/ A motif featuring an elegant impression adorned with picots and popcorn stitches.

270, 271/ The pineapple pattern adds a great accent. This is the true charm of lace designs!

272

273

※ In the 5th round, work the double crochet stitches by picking up between the stitches of the previous round.

274

272/ A motif that evokes traditional Japanese patterns when connected.

273/ Have you ever crocheted so many triple treble crochets at once!?

274/ The picots in the final round resemble petals and are cute.

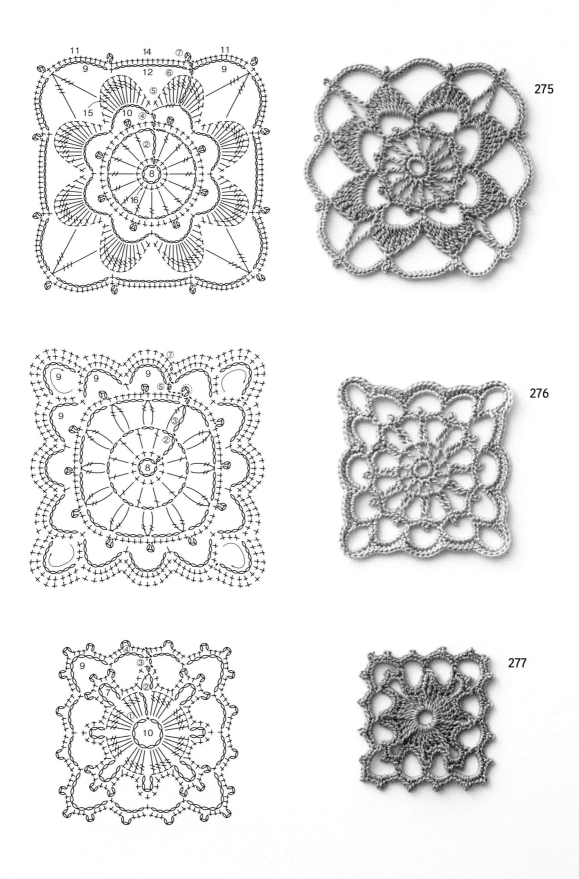

275

276

277

275/ Pay attention to the curve of the petals and be careful with the height of the stitches.

276, 277/ Lace motifs will be much more stable if you tidy up the edges with single crochet stitches.

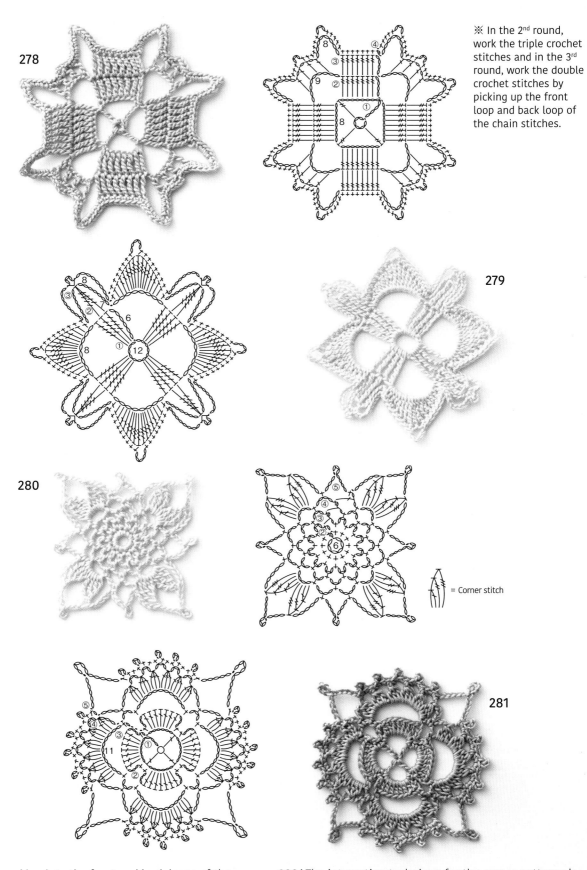

278

279

280

281

※ In the 2nd round, work the triple crochet stitches and in the 3rd round, work the double crochet stitches by picking up the front loop and back loop of the chain stitches.

= Corner stitch

278/ By working into the front and back loops of the chain stitches from the previous round, you get a more structured finish.

279/ A vibrant motif designed with stitches of considerable height.

280/ The interesting technique for the corner patterns is quite enjoyable.

281/ The project is simpler to crochet than it seems, using only basic stitches.

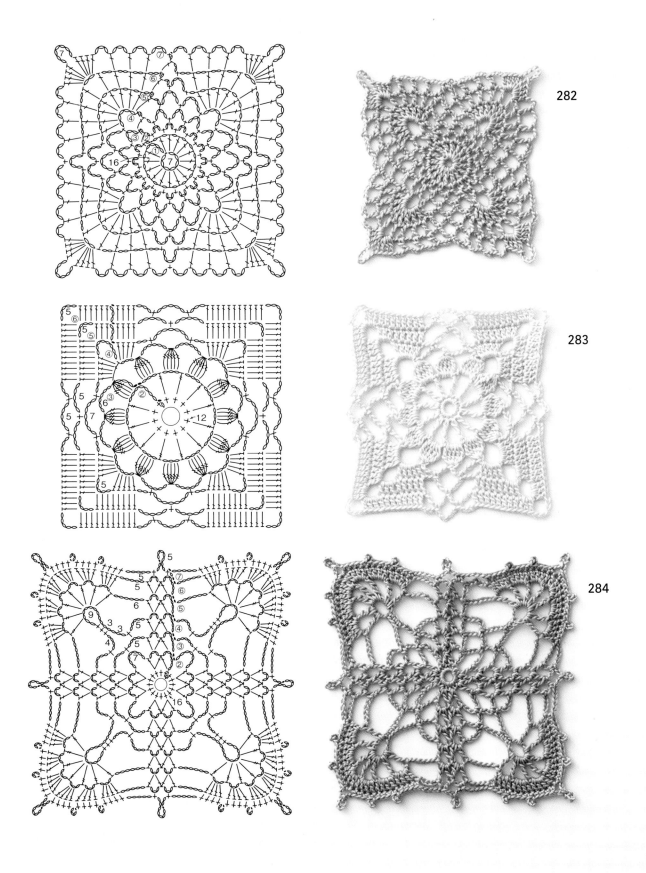

282

283

284

282/ Like butterfly wings! A motif with an elegant impression.

283/ The crochet pattern has a rhythm to it, making it easy to crochet.

284/ This delicate, lacy motif would be ideal for making a shawl or a marguerite.

285/ The contrast between double crochet and mesh stitch is exquisite.

286/ The balancing single crochet and chain stitches is challenging.

287/ The motif, with its ancient design inspiration, is filled with romantic allure.

288/ A neat and clear pattern is achieved by combining double crochet with picots.

289, 290/ Even lacy motifs become stable and easier to crochet when finished with double crochet.

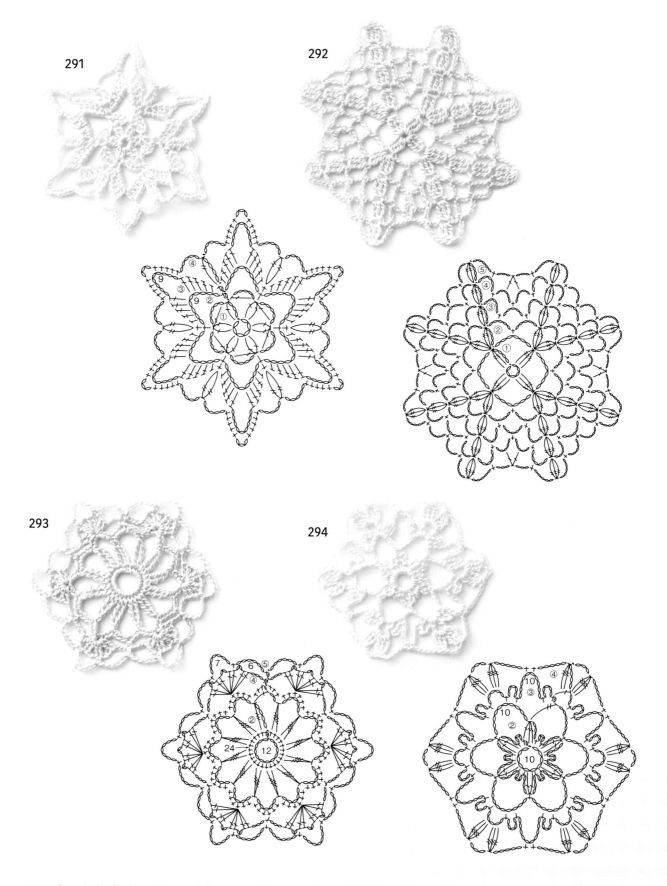

291/ The windmill-shaped central flower motif is ideal for a shawl project.

292/ Connecting the mesh spaces and line patterns could produce an intriguing effect.

293/ The triple treble crochets at the center should maintain the same tension throughout to ensure consistent height.

294/ This delicate lacy flower motif has a breezy and light appearance.

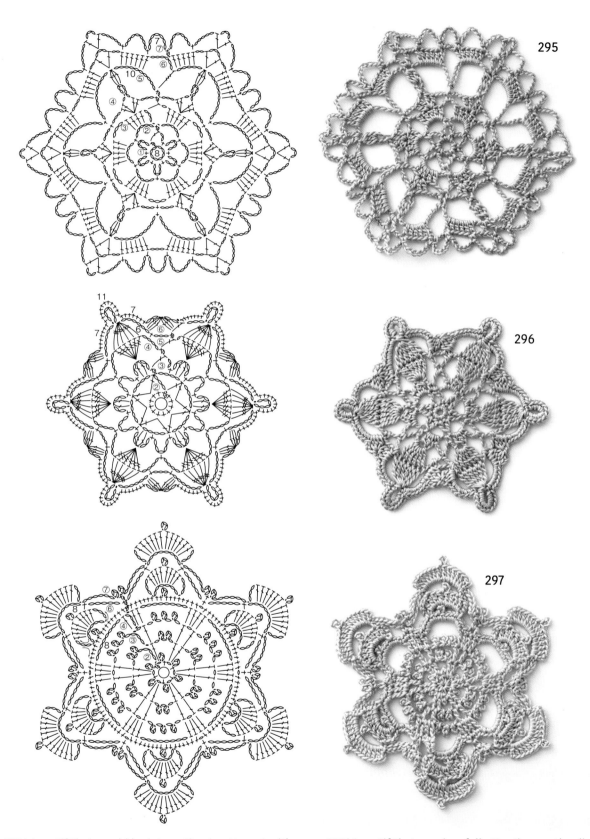

295/ A motif that would be interesting to attempt with continuous crochet.

296/ This arabesque-like design has a striking presence, even as a single motif.

297/ A motif that requires full attention, as the direction of the crochet can reverse.

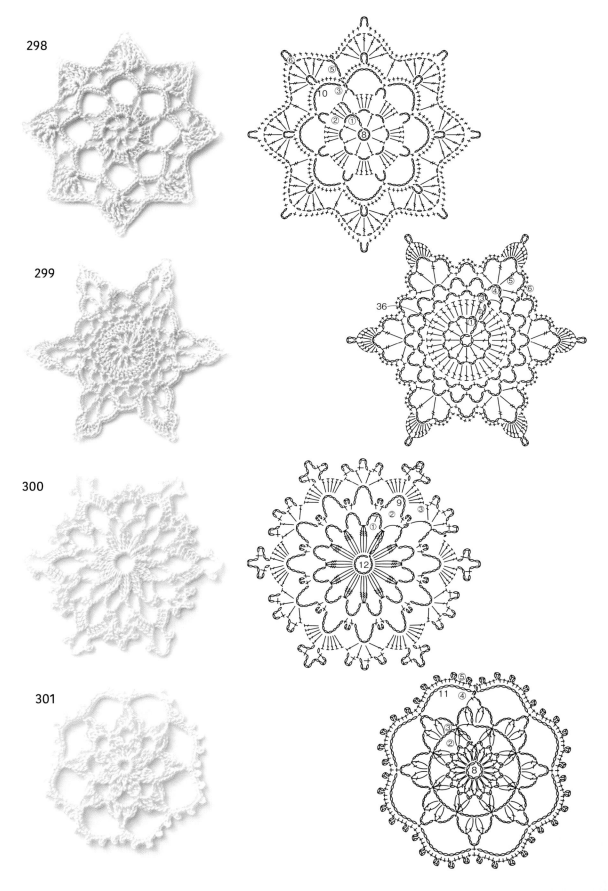

298 The sharpness of the corners will greatly influence the final appearance.

299 A shawl would be lovely to crochet using mohair yarn or similar.

300 This design resembles a snowflake!

301 The picots adorning the edges add a delightful touch.

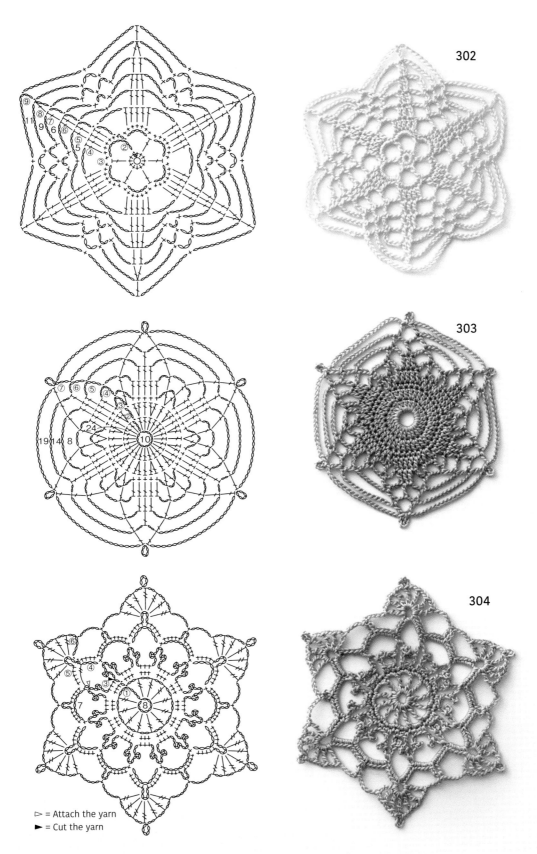

302

303

304

▷ = Attach the yarn
► = Cut the yarn

302, 303/ It's challenging to maintain the shape of motifs based on mesh stitch evenly. Pay attention to keeping the size of the chains consistent.

304/ The pattern in the third round is an adaptation of slip stitch picots worked into the chain stitches.

305/ It's enjoyable to see the pattern spread out gradually.

306/ For the fourth round, the bobble stitches are made by splitting and working into the chains.

307/ The chain stitch pattern in the final round should be crocheted while envisioning the finished shape, and then completed.

308

309

310

308/ Chain stitch patterns are prone to distortion, making it challenging to maintain the shape.

309/ A cheerful pattern resembling a four-leaf clover.

310/ The popcorn stitch of triple treble crochets in the final round can be challenging.

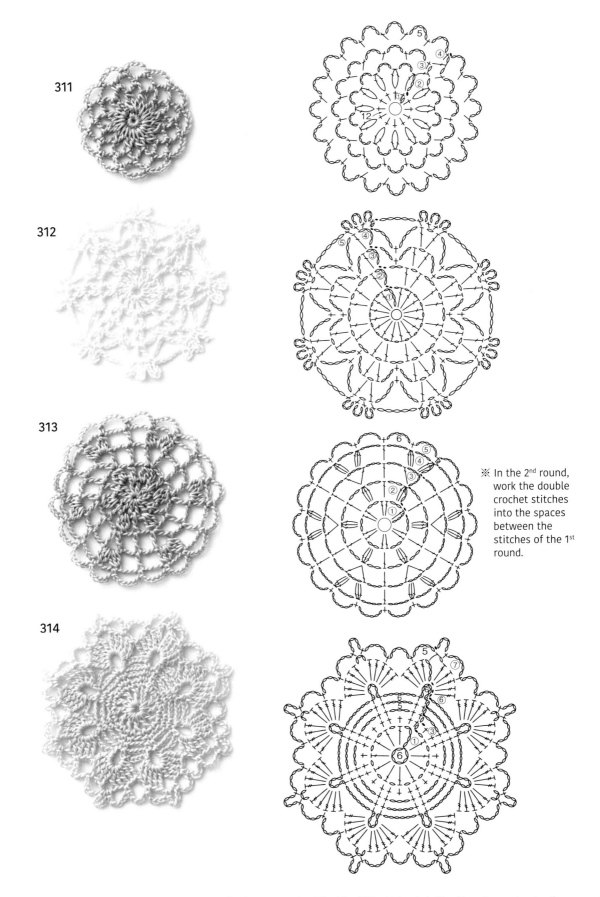

311

312

313

※ In the 2nd round, work the double crochet stitches into the spaces between the stitches of the 1st round.

314

311/ Small and cute. It would be interesting to try crocheting with airy yarns like mohair.

312/ The balance of stitches is easy to manage, making it simple to crochet.

313/ While it's difficult to stabilize the shape due to the many spaces, it's a slightly unusual grid-based circular motif.

314/ The chains forming the central vein pattern should be crocheted tightly for best results.

315 To prevent the legs of the triple-wrapped double crochet from loosening, maintain uniform height while crocheting.

316 The mesh around the edges creates a delicate ruffle pattern.

317 It's inspiring to consider making a mat using craft cord.

318 Pay attention to ensuring the spaces in the chain stitches are even.

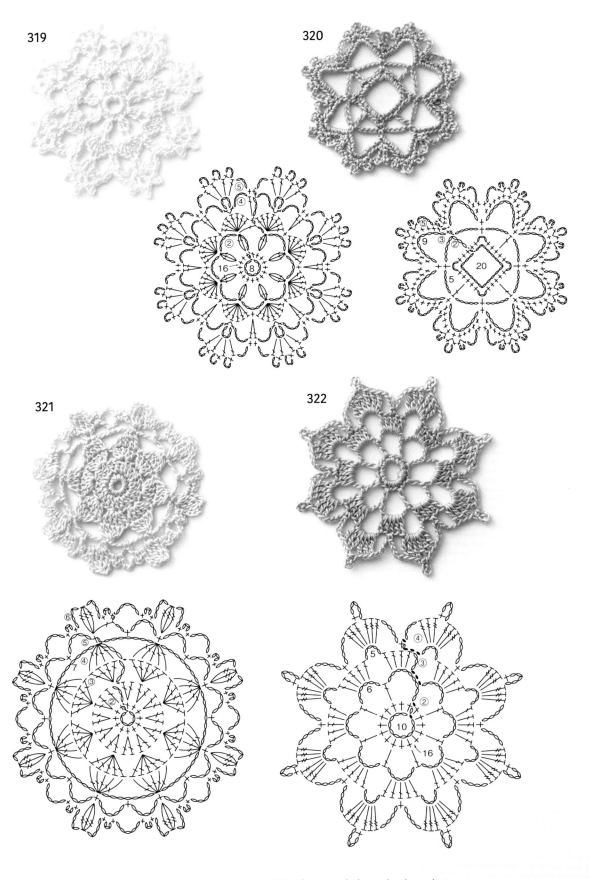

319/ The picot pattern around the edge resembles snowflakes or sparklers.

320/ The central square looks neat when crocheted tightly.

321/ The round shape is charming.

322/ An easy-to-crochet motif that results in a beautiful flower shape.

323 **324** **325** **326**

323/ The picot edging is elegant. It would be fun to try it with colorful color schemes.

324/ Despite the effort required for the many triple crochet bobbles, the completion brings a remarkable sense of achievement.

325/ Pay attention to the height of the stitches when crocheting triple-wrapped double crochet.

326/ The three-picot cluster at the petal tips is charmingly delicate.

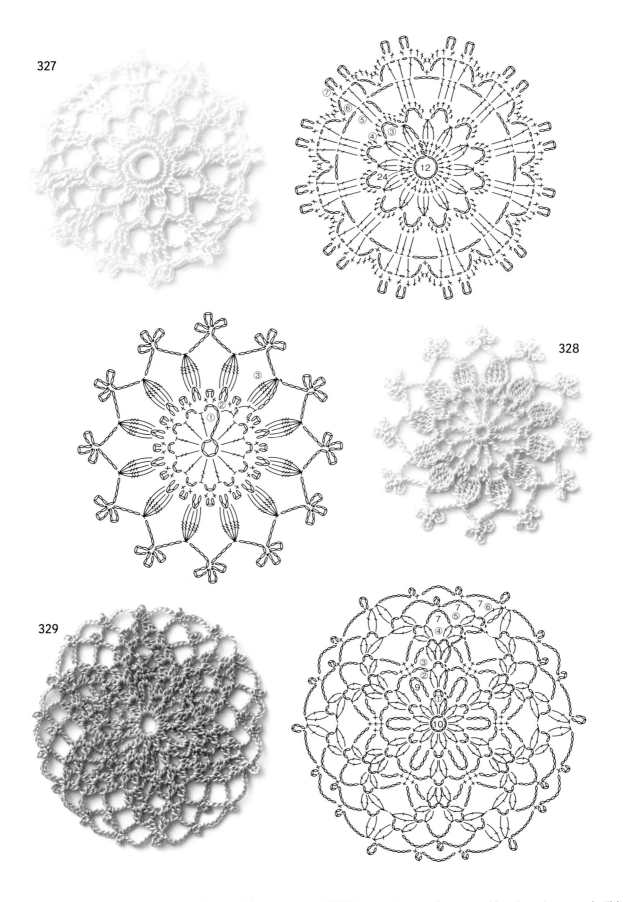

327

328

329

327/ Crocheting the single crochet stitches tightly gives a crisp, structured appearance.

328/ The picots around the edge resemble clovers.

329/ The abundance of picots adds a luxurious touch. This motif would also work well as a coaster.

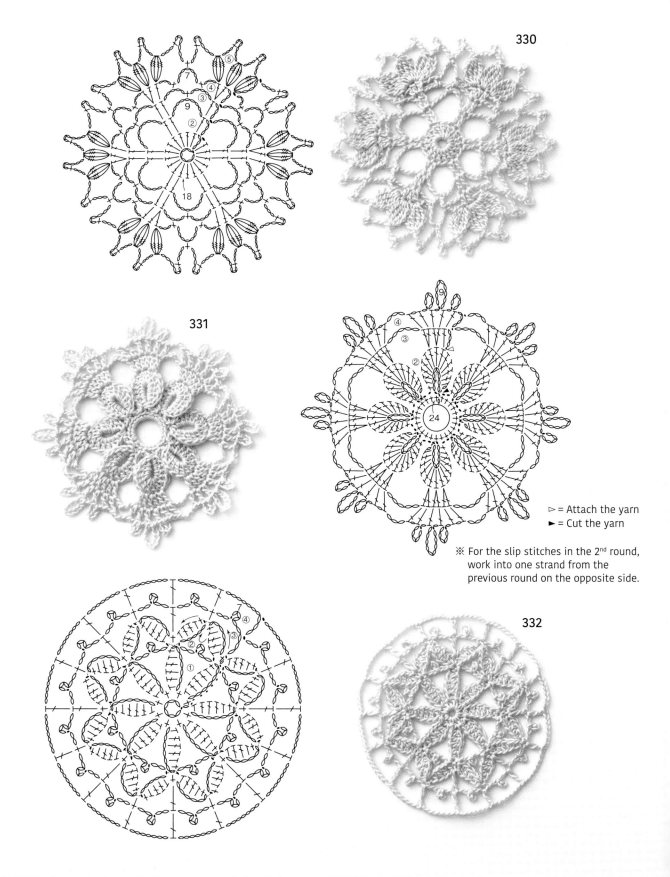

330

331

332

▷ = Attach the yarn
► = Cut the yarn

※ For the slip stitches in the 2ⁿᵈ round,
work into one strand from the
previous round on the opposite side.

330/ The key point in crocheting popcorn stitches is to tighten the top.

331/ When crocheting the petal pattern onto the chain, be careful as the stitches can loosen easily.

332/ This motif, featuring intricate leaf patterns and chain edges prone to distortion, requires advanced skills.

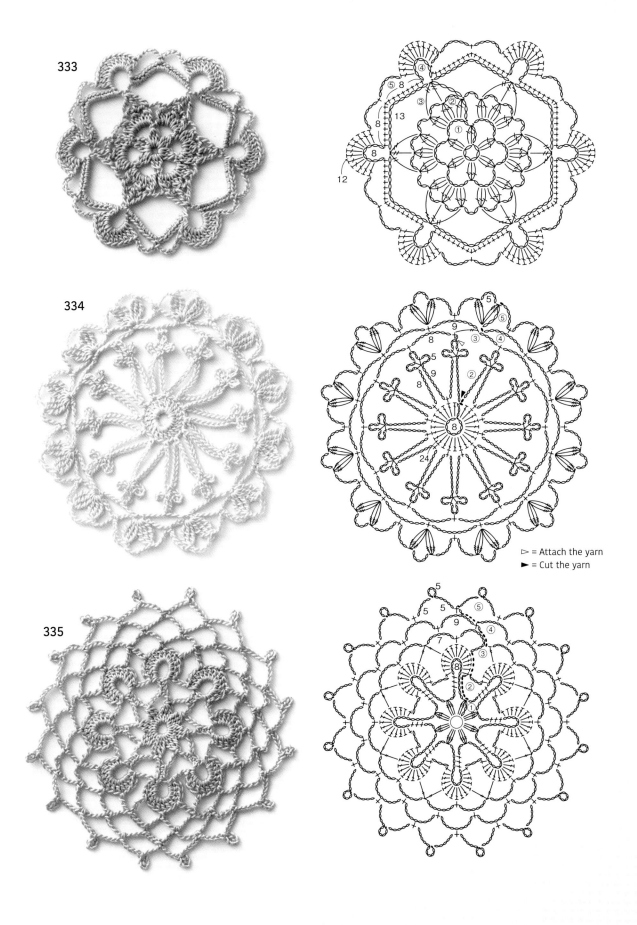

333

334

335

▷ = Attach the yarn
► = Cut the yarn

333/ A stylish pattern resembling antique tile designs.

334/ Pay attention to keeping the chain stitches the same length.

335/ For lace work, the key to beauty is to prevent the bases of the single crochet stitches from loosening.

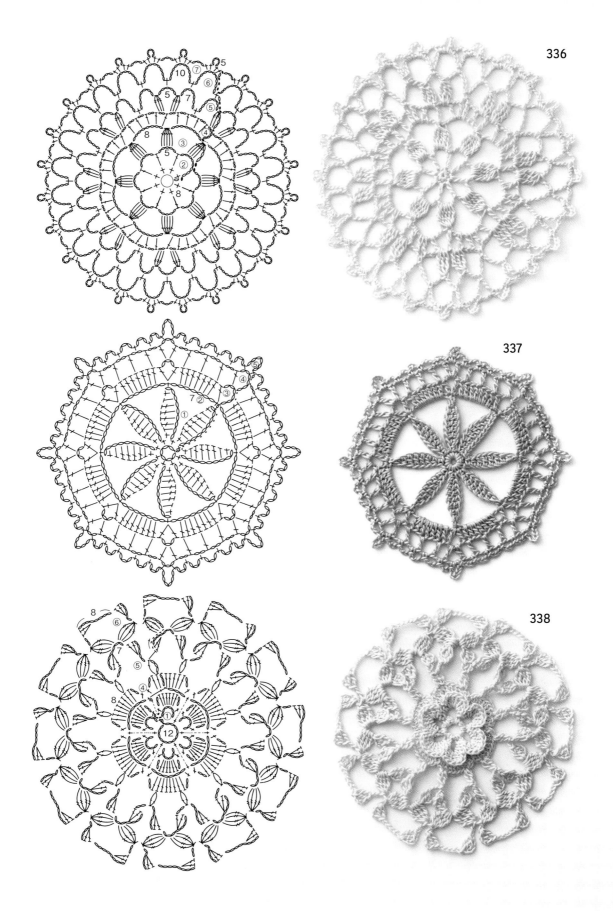

336/ A motif featuring a slightly vintage feel.

337/ A playful design with flowers inserted in the center.

338/ The multiple directions of crocheting make the process enjoyable and varied.

339/ The finely detailed and sizable motif could be used directly as a doily.

340/ The contrast between the bobble petals and the lacework's transparency is exquisite.

341

342

‡ = Pick up the strands
of chain stitches from
the previous and the
round before that, and
work single crochet
into them.

343

341,343/ Be mindful to keep the popcorn stitch size uniform and prevent the stitches from loosening at the beginning.

342/ The picots along the edge are vibrant! It would be great to join them together and make a stole.

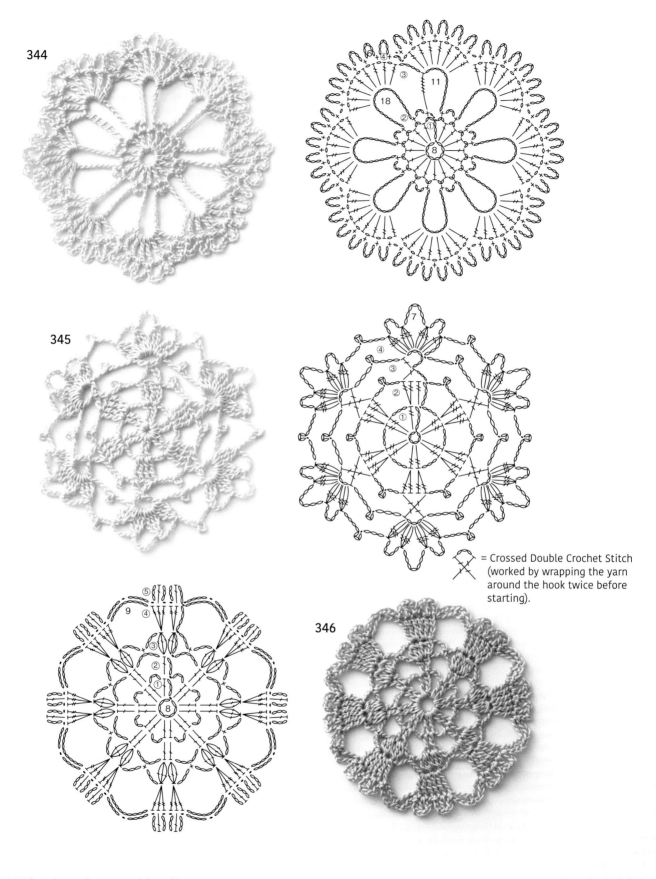

344

345

= Crossed Double Crochet Stitch
(worked by wrapping the yarn
around the hook twice before
starting).

346

344/ The picots that resemble ruffles are charming. Be sure to keep the chain stitch lengths consistent.

345/ Joining these pieces could be ideal for making a bolero or a vest.

346/ They seem to create interesting effects when joined together.

347/ Tighten the tops of the bobbles firmly while crocheting.

348/ Light colors create a subtle appearance, while dark colors produce a stylish effect.

349/ A modern motif with straight and curved lines.

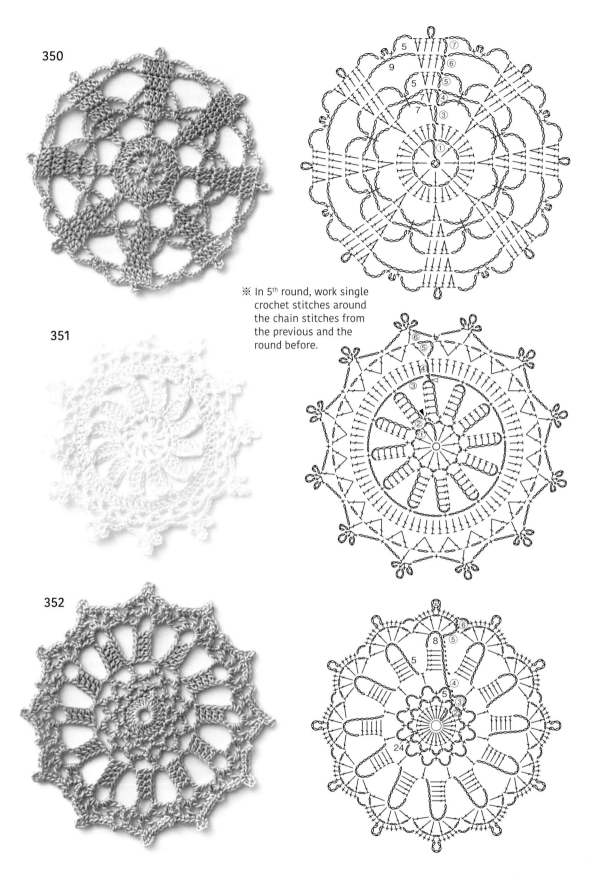

350

351

352

※ In 5th round, work single
crochet stitches around
the chain stitches from
the previous and the
round before.

350, 351, 352/ A set of striking and distinctive motifs! Each one is a fully realized design. Perfect for ornaments!

353 A rustic flower motif with simple double crochets and net stitches. Easy to crochet and recommended for beginners.

354 A lacy zigzag circular motif with a central modified Y-stitch pattern. The fan-shaped design that tilts to either side is distinctive.

355 An embellished version of the motif number 353.

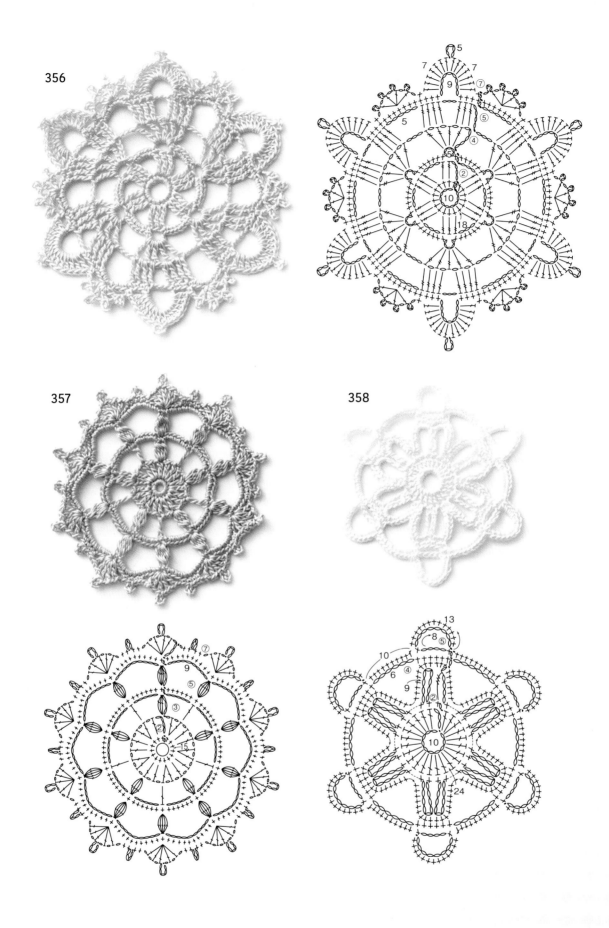

356 / A motif that has a rich, substantial appearance.

357 / Ensure that the size of the puff stitches is consistent.

358 / How cute! Does it look like a turtle to me only?

359

360

361

= Triangle stitch

359/ A motif featuring triangle stitches that is intriguing. Consistent results require practice.

360/ Despite the abundance of double crochets, this motif provides a satisfying challenge while resulting in a stable and beautiful finish.

361/ The spiral pattern created with single crochets and chains is truly beautiful.

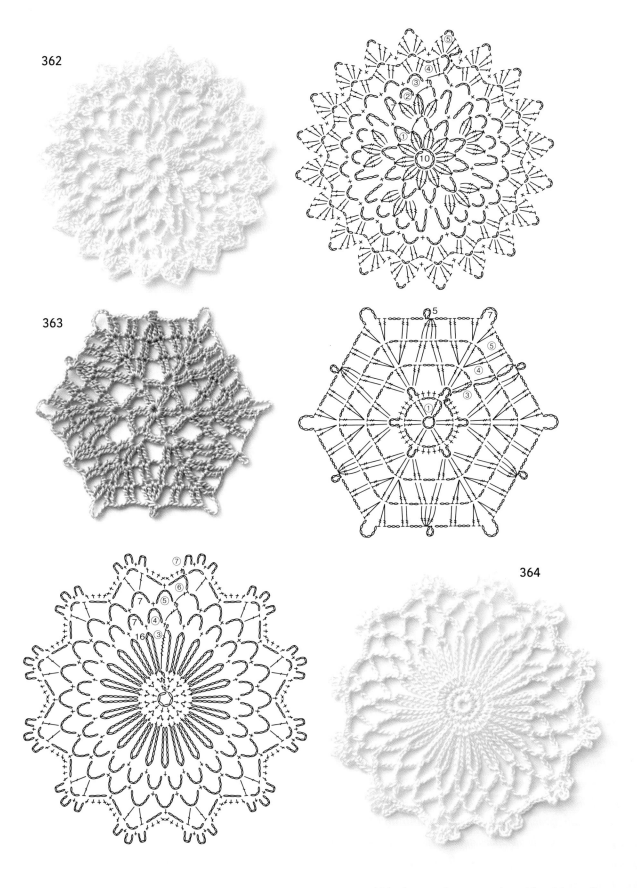

362

363

364

362/ An elegant and vibrant motif with a distinctive presence, reminiscent of a dahlia.

363/ A sharp motif with long double crochet lines that spread out like veins in a leaf.

364/ It would be interesting to crochet this with gradient colors or different color combinations.

365/ A lacey spiral pattern that seems to send a refreshing breeze.

366/ Since the rhythm of the pattern is irregular, pay close attention to the crochet diagram while working. It's a motif that requires constant focus.

How to Join Motifs

There are two ways of joining motifs: by crocheting the motif and joining it afterwards, or by joining the motif at the final stage of crocheting. Choose the most suitable joining method based on the shape of the motif and the crochet pattern.

Joining Motifs Separately

This method involves crocheting the required number of motifs and then joining them all at once later. It works well for shapes with defined edges like triangles, squares, hexagons, and octagons. However, it is less suitable for motifs with network patterns on the final round or for circular or floral shapes. This approach allows for flexibility in arranging colorful motifs, as you can check the placement before joining. Additionally, using different colors for the joining yarn can add an accent to the joining lines.

• Whipstitch

This is the simplest and most convenient method for joining motifs using a tapestry needle. It involves inserting the needle into each pair of adjacent stitches and whipstitching them together to create a neat and secure join.

Half-Stitch Whipstitch

This technique involves using a tapestry needle to whip stitch through the edges of the motifs with a half-stitch approach, ensuring a clean and seamless join. The joining yarn is visible just enough to make a subtle statement, resulting in a seamless and thin join.

 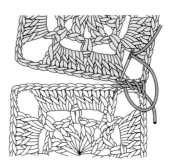

Insert the needle into one outer loop (half-stitch) of each stitch, working in the same direction.

Full-Stitch Whipstitch

In this technique, you join the motifs by whipstitching through every stitch along the edges, ensuring that the joining yarn is visible but blends well with the overall design. Join the motifs by whipstitching through every stitch in the same manner as with half-stitch whipstitch. This method creates a sturdy join.

Insert the needle through both loops of the stitch head (or chain stitches), working in the same direction.

• Slip Stitch

It's simple and quick to complete. When joining motifs with their right sides together and using slip stitches, the seam will be barely visible from the front, making it subtle.

(front)

(back)

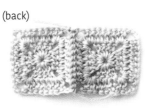

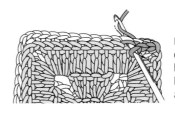

Insert the needle into the outer loop of each stitch (or half-stitch) and pull through, keeping the tension loose to avoid puckering.

Joining as You Go

This method allows for connecting motifs at their points, making it suitable for delicate net patterns, circles, flowers, and also for motifs with well-defined edges. It's a versatile joining technique. Once the motifs are completed, the joining is finished as well. However, mistakes can be challenging to undo later, so planning ahead is essential. Alternatively, a strategy is to leave the final round unfinished on some motifs and then join them all together once you have a complete set. It's also important to join the motifs using the finished edges or netting whenever possible.

Joining with Slip Stitch

Replace the chain stitches in the netting of the motif with slip stitches for joining. This method creates a seamless overlap in the netting.

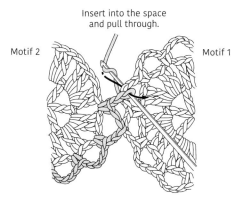

Insert the hook from the front into the space of the first motif and pull through.

Joining with Single Crochet

Replace the chain stitches in the mesh pattern with single crochet stitches to join the motifs. This creates a seamless and natural connection between them.

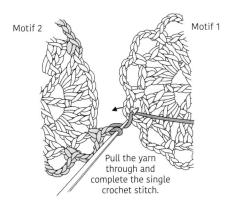

Insert the hook from the back into the space of the first motif, pull the yarn through, and complete a single crochet stitch.

Joining with Double Crochet (top of the stitch)

Join the motifs by connecting the tops of the stitches in the final round. Before creating the joining stitch, insert the hook into the corresponding stitch of the adjacent motif and then complete the stitch.

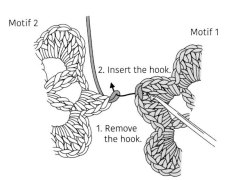

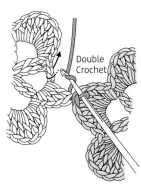

1 Remove the hook from the second motif, insert it into the top of the double crochet on the first motif, and pull the loop through.

2 Continue crocheting the double crochet stitch on the second motif.

Variations in Joining Motifs

While completing a single motif can be satisfying at first, the real fun begins when connecting multiple motifs. Interestingly, even the same motif can create various effects depending on the arrangement, leading to unexpected results. By connecting your favorite motifs in a way that suits your taste, you can enjoy creating original pieces.

Square Motifs

Joining Straight

Align and join the edges evenly.

Motif 256/ Page 80

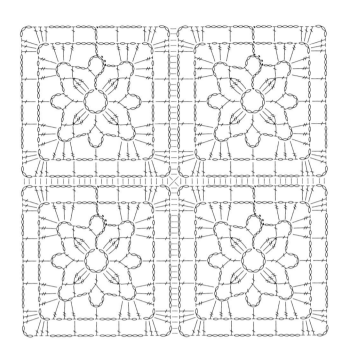

Joining Diagonally

Filling the space with small motifs will stabilize the crocheted fabric.

Motif 279 / Page 88

118

Joining Straight

If you fill the space with small motifs, the crocheted fabric becomes stable.

Motif 34 8/ Page 109

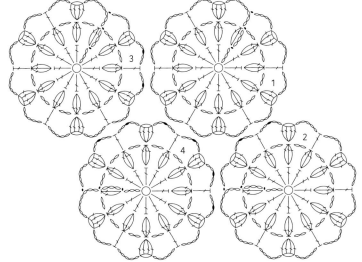

Joining Alternately

Aligning the peaks and valleys of the motifs allows for a seamless connection.

Motif 202 / 65 pages

Joining the Tips

Joining at the tips of the petals or the corners of the motifs creates a design with a delicate, airy look.

Motif 121 / Page 42

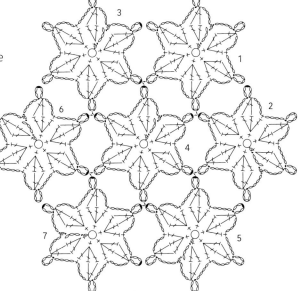

Triangle Motif

Joining the Top and Bottom Edges in an Alternating Pattern

Arrange the peaks and bases of the triangular motifs alternately to join them into a strip. (The number of chain stitches at the corners is adjusted for joining.)

Motif 80/ Page 28

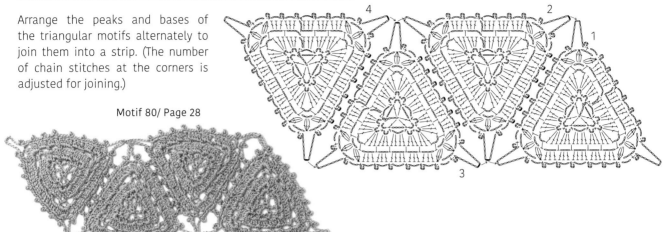

Joining the Corners and Edges Together

By aligning the edges around the vertices of the triangles, a hexagonal surface is created. This technique is suitable for items like bag bottoms or doilies. (The motifs are in color variation.)

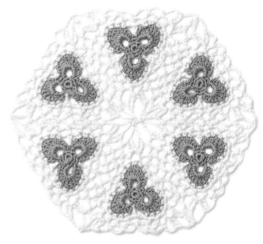

Motif 88 / Page 31

Joining the Corners Directly

Align the tips of the corners. When the space is large, you can also fill in the gaps with small motifs.

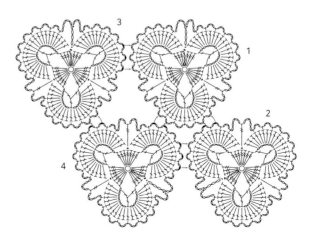

Motif 87 / Page 30

Garments and Accessories Made with Joined Motifs

This book showcases how to expand the motifs into finished pieces. Once you find your favorite motif, think about what to make next. What kind of yarn to use, how to arrange the motifs—just imagining it is exciting!

Flat Tote Bag

A natural-colored bag with navy handles creates a sleek and refreshing design. Basic motifs are crocheted in advance and then quickly joined using slip stitches. You can customize the bag by making it smaller or larger, or even elongating it horizontally to suit your preferences.

Yarn: Puppy Leafy (Paper Yarn)
Motif: 6 / Page 8
Instructions: Page 131

Trapezoidal Shawl

A large, elegant shawl in soft beige and off-white hues. The final round of motifs features a shell pattern that has been adapted to finish the edges. This versatile piece is perfect for the chilly early spring or as a cooling layer in summer air conditioning.

Yarn: Diamond Masterseed Cotton
Motif: 95 / Page 33
Instructions: Page 132

Collar

A delicate collar adorned with 63 small flowers. Add small flower motifs to the spaces along the neckline where the main motifs are joined, creating a gentle curve. Small crochet beads are attached to the front to fasten it. A ribbon can be added using crochet ties for a charming touch.

Yarn: Olympus Emmy Grande
Motif: 215 / Page 68
Instructions: Page 134

Colorful Scarf

The charmingly puffed stitches of this motif stand out against a black base, with vibrant, pop colors adding a lively touch! The cluster stitches of half double crochet maintain their appearance on both sides, making them perfect for a scarf. This accessory is great for adding a playful element to your everyday outfits.

Yarn: Ski Tasmanian Polowarth
Motif: 217 / Page 69
Instructions: Page 135

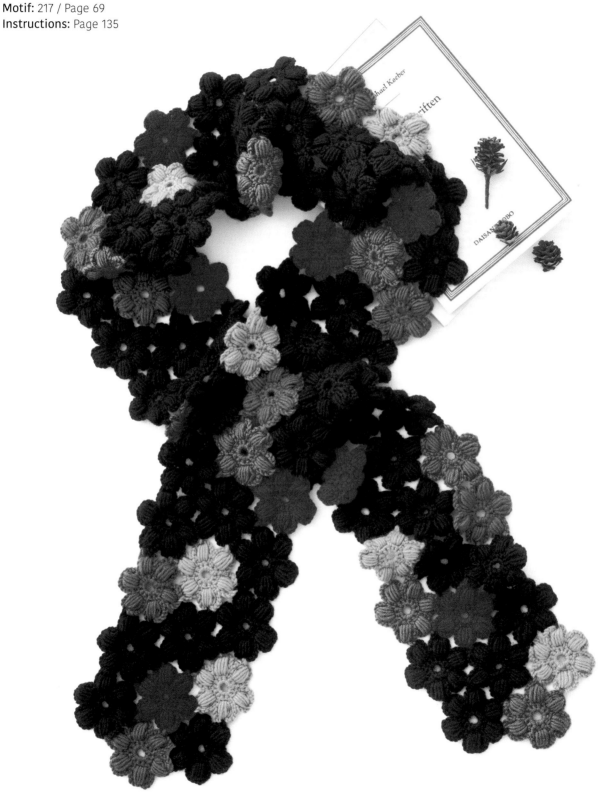

Drawstring Bag

Hexagon motifs are joined together to form a circular shape, with the top edge finished with a border. This round drawstring bag features a retro-modern monochrome look in white and black. It's a versatile motif that would be great in various color schemes, from natural to traditional styles.

Yarn: Hamanaka Wash Cotton
Motif: 70 / Page 26
Instructions: Page 136

Bolero

This short bolero is made by simply joining motifs in straight lines for both the body and sleeves. The design has no edging, making the finished piece delightfully easy to complete. With its simple construction, it's easy to adjust the width, hem, and sleeve length to fit your size, or to experiment with different motifs.

Yarn: Olympus Emmy Grande
Motif: 259 / Page 81
Instructions: Page 140

Pullover

This pullover in vivid pink brightens the wearer's appearance with its impactful color. It's ideal as an accent in a simple outfit. As the motifs are joined together, new patterns emerge, showcasing the charm of motifs!

Yarn: Puppy Cotton Kona Fine
Motif: 257 / Page 81
Instructions: Page 138

Baby Cap

A cute baby hat adorned with pom-poms. The design features motifs of different sizes to match its look. Made with a soft yarn, it's perfect for walks and outdoor play throughout the year. It also makes a delightful gift when you make several.

Yarn: Hamanaka Paume Baby Color
Motif: 1, 5 / Page 8
Instructions: Page 129

a

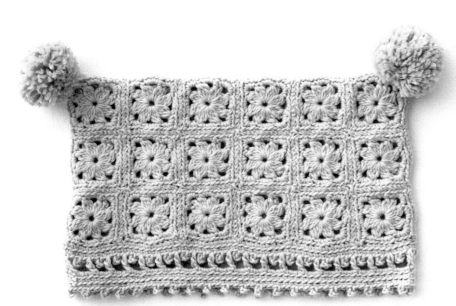

b

[a] Use **Motif 1**, **[b]** Use **Motif 5** from Page 8

► **MATERIALS**

Hamanaka Paume Baby Color [Crochet]
- [a] Cream (603) 30g/2 balls
- [b] Blue (605) 35g/2 balls

► **TOOLS**

Crochet Hook: Size 2.5mm

► **FINISHED MEASUREMENTS**
- [a] Head circumference 39cm, depth 15.3cm
- [b] Head circumference 39cm, depth 12.75cm

► **GAUGE**
- [a] One side of the motif measures 3.9cm
- [b] One side of the motif measures 3.25cm

Points for Crocheting

After crocheting the specified number of motifs, refer to the chart and join them using the half stitch whipstitch.

- [a] For the top, pick up the specified number of stitches from the joined motifs and work in the pattern. Follow the chart for decreases. Finish by inserting the hook into the stitches of the final round, pulling the yarn through every other stitch to gather. Pick up stitches from the opposite side of the motif joining and crochet the edging in the round. Finish by adding a pom-pom to the top.

- [b] Refer to the chart to pick up stitches from the opening and crochet the edging in the round. Add two pom-poms to the corners of the top to finish.

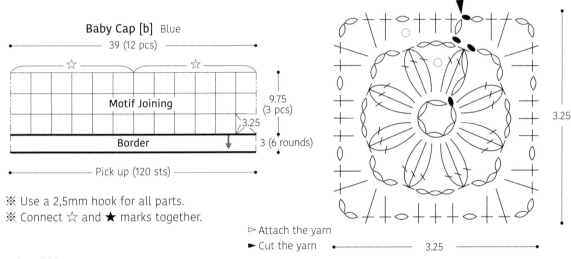

Baby Cap [b] Blue

— 39 (12 pcs) —

Motif Joining

Border

9.75 (3 pcs)

3.25

3 (6 rounds)

— Pick up (120 sts) —

※ Use a 2,5mm hook for all parts.
※ Connect ☆ and ★ marks together.

▷ Attach the yarn
► Cut the yarn

3.25

3.25

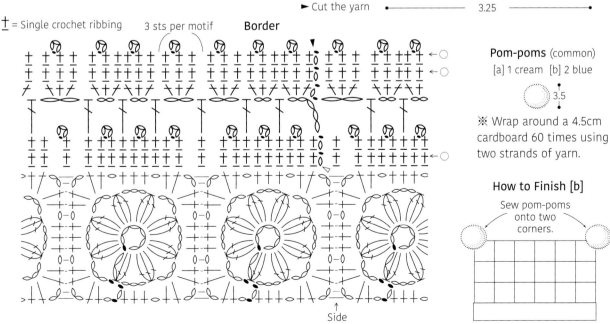

$\dagger$ = Single crochet ribbing

3 sts per motif

Border

← ○
← ○

← ○

> Side

Pom-poms (common)

[a] 1 cream [b] 2 blue

3.5

※ Wrap around a 4.5cm cardboard 60 times using two strands of yarn.

How to Finish [b]

Sew pom-poms onto two corners.

Baby Cap [a] Cream

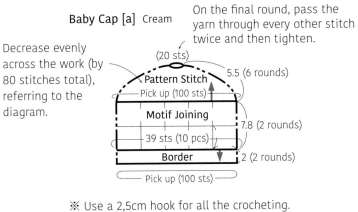

On the final round, pass the yarn through every other stitch twice and then tighten.

Decrease evenly across the work (by 80 stitches total), referring to the diagram.

(20 sts)
Pattern Stitch
Pick up (100 sts)
5.5 (6 rounds)
Motif Joining
7.8 (2 rounds)
39 sts (10 pcs)
Border
2 (2 rounds)
Pick up (100 sts)

※ Use a 2,5cm hook for all the crocheting.

▷ Attach the yarn
► Cut the yarn

Motif 20 pcs

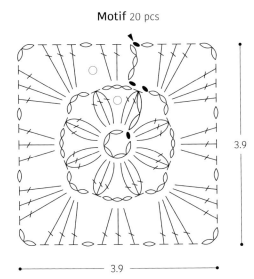

3.9

3.9

Pattern Stitch

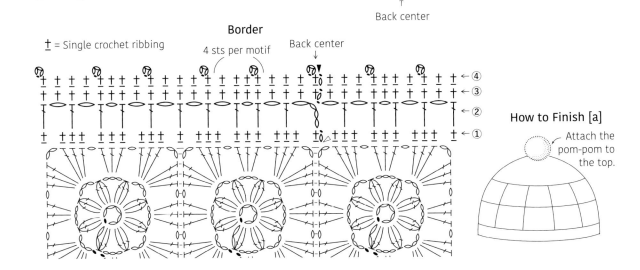

Repeat

← ⑥ (- 10 sts) (20 sts)
← ⑤ (- 10 sts) (30 sts)
← ④ (- 10 sts) (40 sts)
← ③ (- 10 sts) (60 sts)
← ② (- 10 sts) (60 sts)
← ① (100 sts)

Back center

Border

$\underline{+}$ = Single crochet ribbing

4 sts per motif

Back center

← ④
← ③
← ②
← ①

How to Finish [a]

Attach the pom-pom to the top.

130

Use **Motif 6** from Page 8

▸ **MATERIALS**
Puppy Leafy (Paper Yarn)
• Beige (761) 50g/2 balls
• Navy (763) 20g/1 ball

▸ **TOOLS**
Crochet Hooks: Size 3 mm, 3.5 mm

▸ **FINISHED MEASUREMENTS**
Width 22cm, Depth 28.5cm

▸ **GAUGE**
One side of the motif measures 5.5cm.

Key Points for Crocheting
You will crochet the specified number of motifs. Align the motifs with their right sides facing each other, and use the designated color to join them together from the back with a slip stitch. Crochet a round of single crochet around the opening. Pick up stitches from the specified positions to crochet the handles. Finish the project by following the diagram for final touches.

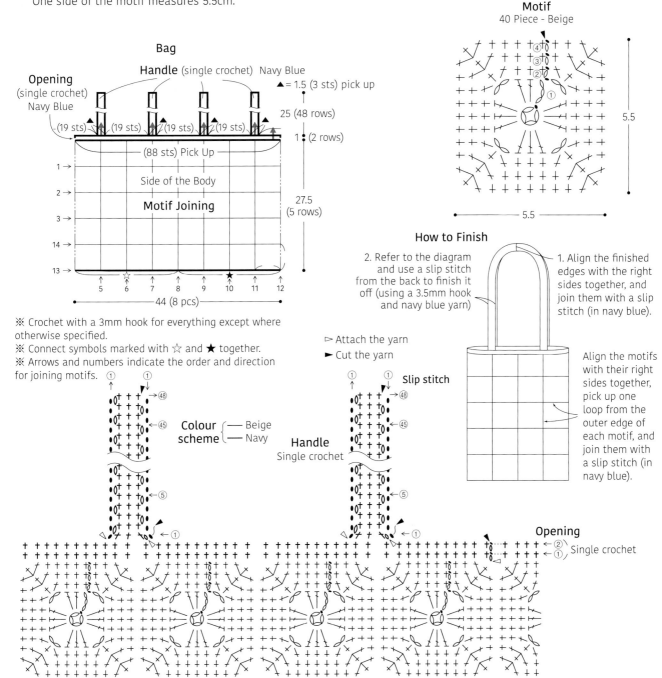

Bag

Opening (single crochet) Navy Blue

Handle (single crochet) Navy Blue

▲ = 1.5 (3 sts) pick up

25 (48 rows)

-(19 sts) ▲ (19 sts) (19 sts) (19 sts)

1 (2 rows)

(88 sts) Pick Up

Side of the Body

Motif Joining

27.5 (5 rows)

44 (8 pcs)

Motif
40 Piece - Beige

5.5

5.5

How to Finish

2. Refer to the diagram and use a slip stitch from the back to finish it off (using a 3.5mm hook and navy blue yarn)

1. Align the finished edges with the right sides together, and join them with a slip stitch (in navy blue).

Align the motifs with their right sides together, pick up one loop from the outer edge of each motif, and join them with a slip stitch (in navy blue).

Opening

※ Crochet with a 3mm hook for everything except where otherwise specified.
※ Connect symbols marked with ☆ and ★ together.
※ Arrows and numbers indicate the order and direction for joining motifs.

▷ Attach the yarn
► Cut the yarn

Colour scheme — Beige — Navy

Slip stitch

Handle
Single crochet

Opening
Single crochet

※ Crochet the opposite side in the same manner.

131

Use **Motif 95** from Page 33

► **MATERIALS**
Diamond Masterseed Cotton [Crochet]
• Cream (301) 120g/4 balls
• Beige (302) 65g/3 balls

► **TOOLS**
Crochet Hook: Size 2mm

► **FINISHED MEASUREMENTS**
Width 44cm, Length 130cm

► **GAUGE**
Motif diameter is 8cm.

> ## Key Points for Crocheting
> Crochet by joining motifs together. Refer to the diagram for the color scheme, and for each motif after the first, join it to the adjacent motif during the final round. Crochet a single round of edging around the entire piece.

Shawl - Motif Joining

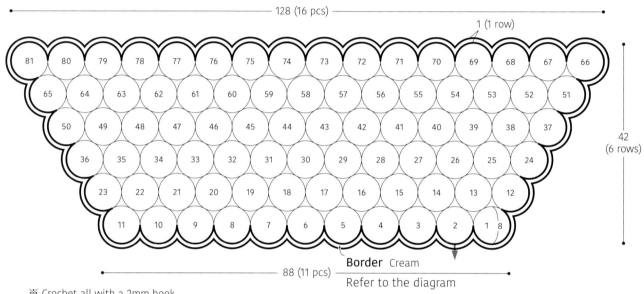

※ Crochet all with a 2mm hook.
※ Numbers within motifs indicate the order for joining them.

Motif 81 pcs

Motif Colour Scheme	
Rounds 1-4	Rounds 5-6
Beige	Cream

▷ = Attach the yarn
► = Cut the yarn

How to Join the Motifs and Add the Edging

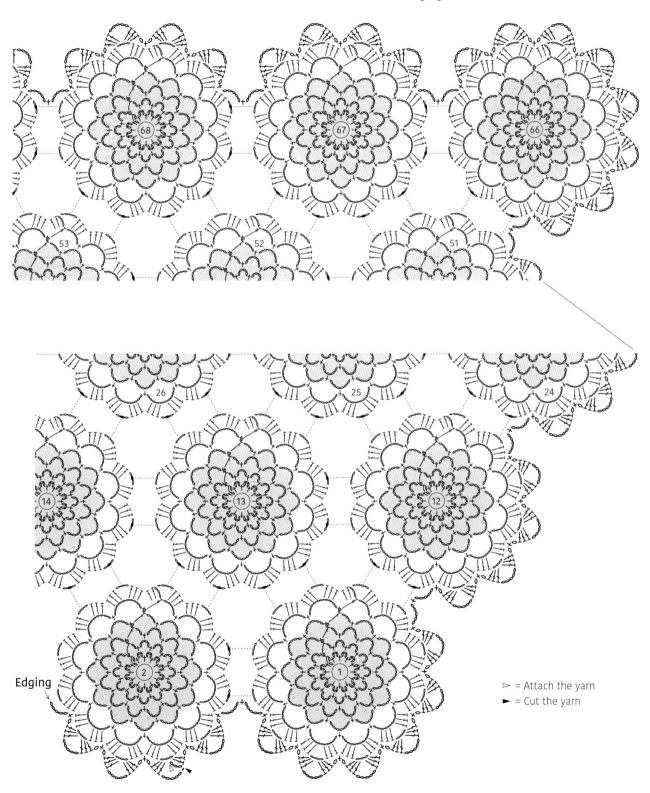

▷ = Attach the yarn
► = Cut the yarn

Edging

Use **Motif 215** from Page 68

▶ **MATERIALS**
Olympus Emmy Grande
• Cream (804) 35g/1 ball

▶ **TOOLS**
Crochet Hook: Size 2mm

▶ **FINISHED MEASUREMENTS**
Collar width: 7.5cm
Neck circumference: 59cm

▶ **GAUGE**
Refer to the diagram for motif size.

Key Points for Crocheting
Crochet all pieces by joining motifs. For each motif after the first, join it to the adjacent motif during the final round. Attach Motif B along the neck edge as you crochet. Make a button and attach it to the designated button position. Use the spaces in the pattern for the buttonhole.

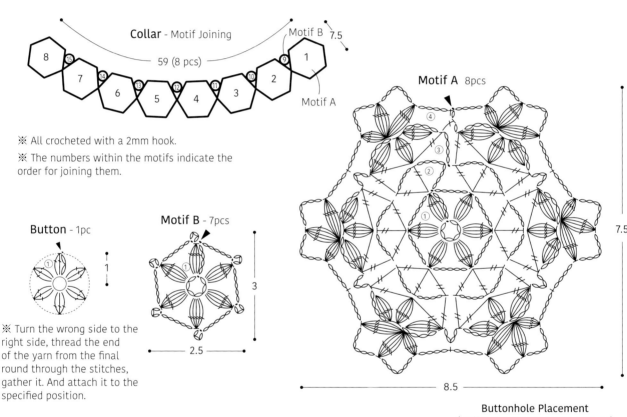

Collar - Motif Joining

Motif B 7.5
Motif A
59 (8 pcs)

※ All crocheted with a 2mm hook.

※ The numbers within the motifs indicate the order for joining them.

Button - 1pc

※ Turn the wrong side to the right side, thread the end of the yarn from the final round through the stitches, gather it. And attach it to the specified position.

Motif B - 7pcs

3

2.5

Motif A 8pcs

7.5

8.5

Button Placement

How to Join the Motifs

Buttonhole Placement
(Utilize the spaces in the pattern)

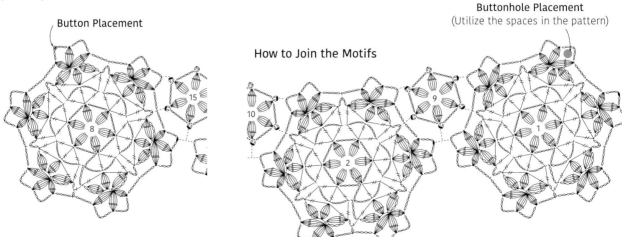

Use **Motif 217** from Page 6.

► **MATERIALS**
Ski Tasmanian Polwarth
• Black (7028) 80g/2 balls
• Moss Green (7021) 15g/1 ball
• Turquoise Blue (7009)
• Ash Pink (7011)
• Brick Red (7013) 10g each / 1 ball

► **TOOLS**
Crochet Hook: Size 3.5mm

► **FINISHED MEASUREMENTS**
Width 12.5cm, Length 139.5cm

► **GAUGE**
Refer to the diagram for motif size.

Key Points for Crocheting

Choose and arrange the colors of the motifs randomly according to your preference. From the second motif onward, join each new motif to the adjacent one during the final round using slip stitches. The puff stitches made with half double crochet should look the same on both the front and back.

How to Join the Motifs

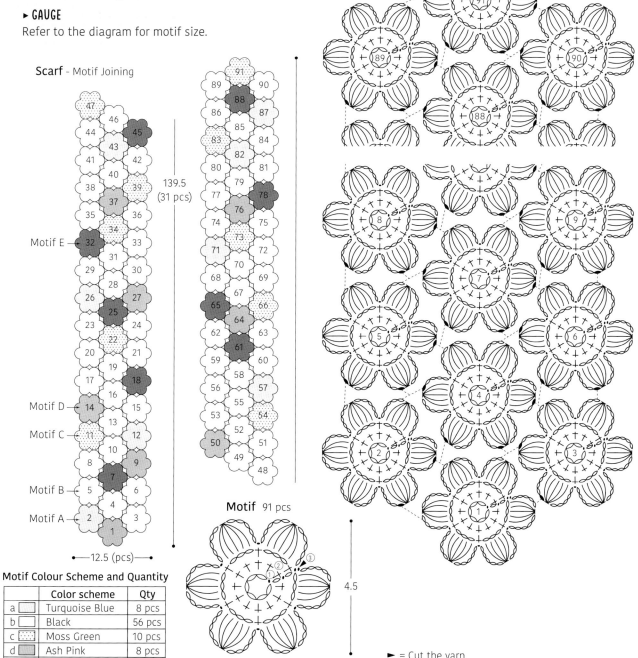

Scarf - Motif Joining

139.5 (31 pcs)

Motif E
Motif D
Motif C
Motif B
Motif A

12.5 (pcs)

Motif 91 pcs

4.5

5

► = Cut the yarn

Motif Colour Scheme and Quantity

	Color scheme	Qty
a	Turquoise Blue	8 pcs
b	Black	56 pcs
c	Moss Green	10 pcs
d	Ash Pink	8 pcs
e	Brick Red	9 pcs

135

Use **Motif 70** from Page 26

▸ **MATERIALS**
Hamanaka Wash Cotton [Crochet]
• Black (120) 30g/2 balls
• White (101) 20g/1 ball

▸ **TOOLS**
Crochet Hook: Size 2mm

▸ **FINISHED MEASUREMENTS**
Bottom diameter 13cm
Depth 6cm (actual measurement)

▸ **GAUGE**
Refer to the diagram for motif size.

Key Points for Crocheting
Crochet by joining motifs together. From the second motif onward, join each new motif to the adjacent one during the final round. For the opening, refer to the diagram to pick up stitches from the motifs and crochet the edging in back-and-forth rounds. Make two cords, thread them through the third round of the edging, and finish by attaching tassels to both ends of the cords.

Drawstring Pouch - Motif Joining

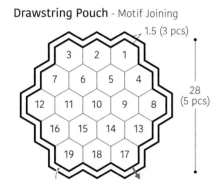

1.5 (3 pcs)

3	2	1
7	6	5	4
12	11	10	9	8
16	15	14	13
19	18	17

28 (5 pcs)

Edging - Black Refer to the diagram
※ Pick up a total of 30 motifs.
← 30 (5 pcs) →

※ All crocheted with a 2mm hook.
※ Numbers within the motifs indicate the order for joining them.

Tassel Ornament - 2 pcs Black

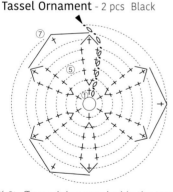

※ Stuff remaining yarn inside the tassel.

Motif 19 pcs

7

6

Color Scheme {— Black / — White}

▷ = Attach the yarn
► = Cut the yarn

Edging

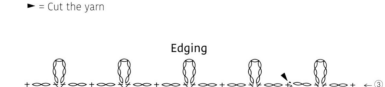

← ③
→ ②
← ①

1 pattern

Increase and Decrease Stitch Counts for the Tassel Ornament

Number of Round	Stitch Count
Round 7	3 sts
Round 6	6 sts
Round 5	12 sts
Round 4	12 sts
Round 3	12 sts
Round 2	12 sts
Round 1	6 sts

Cord
(Thread/Cord) 2 Strands Black

How to Finish
1. Pass through the cord threading position.
Cord
2. Insert into the tassel ornament, stuffing the remaining yarn inside.
Tassel ornament
3. Use the tail end of the yarn to sew and secure the cord.
2

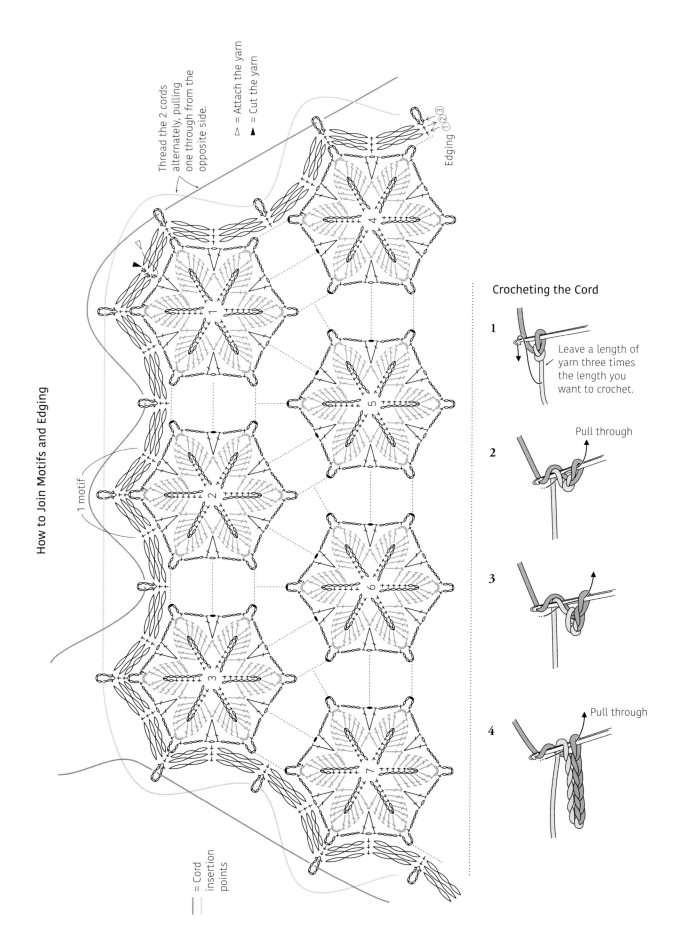

How to Join Motifs and Edging

Thread the 2 cords alternately, pulling one through from the opposite side.

△ = Attach the yarn
▲ = Cut the yarn

Edging ①②③

1 motif

= Cord insertion points

Crocheting the Cord

1 Leave a length of yarn three times the length you want to crochet.

2 Pull through

3

4 Pull through

Use **Motif 257** from Page 81

▶ **MATERIALS**
Puppy Cotton Kona Fine
• Magenta (353) 2459/10 skeins

▶ **TOOLS**
Crochet Hook: Size 1.75mm

▶ **FINISHED MEASUREMENTS**
Bust 88 cm
Length 39cm
Sleeve Length 38,5 cm

▶ **GAUGE**
The side of th each motif
measures 11cm.

Key Points for Crocheting
Crochet by joining motifs together. From the second motif onward, join each new motif to the adjacent one during the final round. For the hem and sleeve cuffs, refer to the diagram to tidy up the edges. Crochet the hem and sleeves in rounds using the pattern stitches. Crochet the collar in rounds using the edging technique.

Motif Joining 34 pcs

► = Cut the yarn

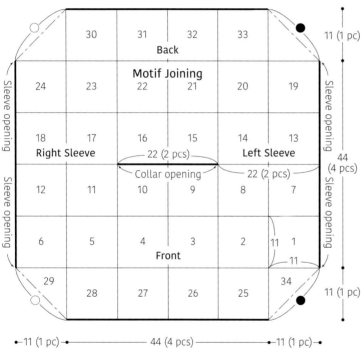

※ All crocheted with lace hook size 1.75 mm.
※ The numbers within the motifs indicate the order for joining them.

Pattern Stitches (hem and sleeve cuffs)

4 stitches per pattern

⌷ = Front Post Treble Crochet Stitch
⌷ = Back Post Treble Crochet Stitch

※ Finish the sleeve cuffs
in the same manner.

Chart 2
How to Finish the Edges of the Motif (Hem)

How to Join the Motifs

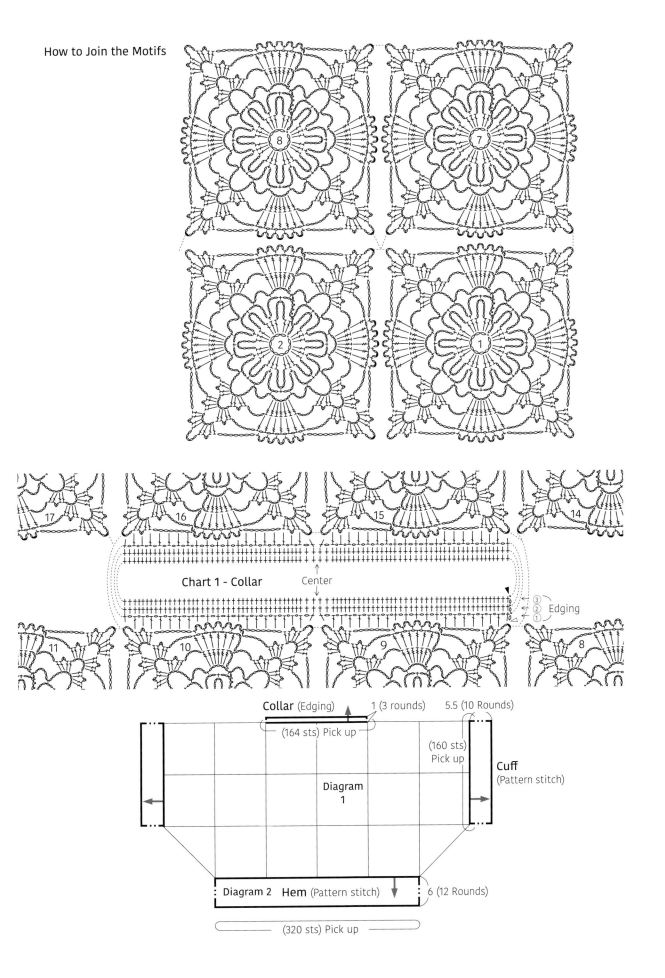

Chart 1 - Collar

Center

Edging
③
②
①

Collar (Edging)   1 (3 rounds)   5.5 (10 Rounds)
(164 sts) Pick up

(160 sts)
Pick up

Cuff
(Pattern stitch)

Diagram
1

Diagram 2   Hem (Pattern stitch)   6 (12 Rounds)

(320 sts) Pick up

Use **Motif 259** from Page 81

▶ **MATERIALS**
Olympus Emmy Grande
• Silver White (481) 290g/6 balls.

▶ **TOOLS**
Lace Hook: Size 1.75mm

▶ **FINISHED MEASUREMENTS**
Length 28cm, Sleeve length 59.5cm.

▶ **GAUGE**
One side of the motif measures 7cm.

> ## Key Points for Crocheting
> Crochet both the body and sleeves entirely by joining motifs together. From the second motif onward, join each new motif to the adjacent one during the final round.

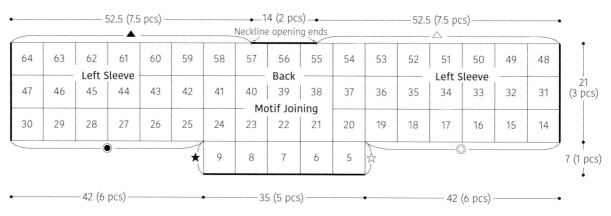

※ All to be crocheted with lace hook size 1.75 mm.
※ The numbers within motifs indicate the order for joining them.
※ Join the motifs marked with matching symbols together.

Motif 124 pcs

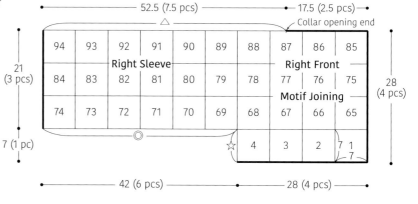

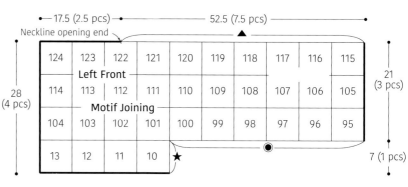

How to Join the Motifs

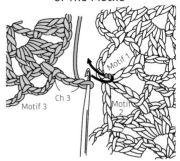

1 To join the third motif, crochet 3 chain stitches at the joining position. Then, insert the hook from above into the two slip stitch legs of the second motif.

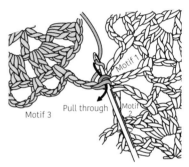

2 Yarn over and pull through. Join the fourth motif in the same position.

Neckline

Neckline opening ends

Back center

Technique Guide

Chain-3 Picot

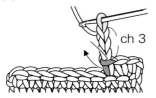 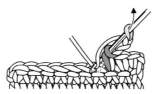  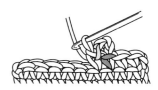

1 After a single crochet, make 3 chain stitches, then insert the hook into the front loop of the first half stitch of the single crochet, and into one strand of the yarn at the base.

2 Yarn over and pull through as indicated by the arrow.

3 Completion of the chain 3 picot.

5 Worked the next single crochet.

Chain-3 Picot (worked into chain stitch)

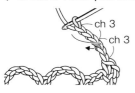  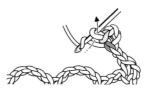 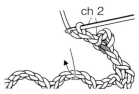

1 After chaining 3 stitches, continue by crocheting 3 more chains. Insert the hook into the half double crochet in the 4th chain from the hook and into the back loop.

2 Yarn over and pull through as indicated by the arrow.

3 In the middle of the chain stitch, a chain-3 picot has been made.

4 Just worked the next 2 chain stitches.

Front Post Double Crochet

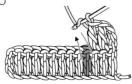 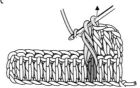

1 Yarn over the hook, insert the hook from the front as if scooping up the entire leg of the previous double crochet stitch, and bring it forward.

2 Yarn over, pull through a longer loop, then work a double crochet stitch.

Back Post Double Crochet

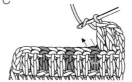 

1 Yarn over the hook, insert the hook from the opposite side as if scooping up the entire leg of the previous double crochet stitch, and bring it through to the opposite side.

2 Yarn over, pull up a loop to make it longer, then work a double crochet stitch.

5-Double Crochet Popcorn Stitch

  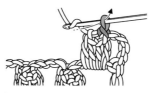 

1 Work 5 double crochet stitches into the space under the chain from the previous row.

2 Remove the hook for a moment, then insert it from the front into the top of the first double crochet stitch, and pull up a loop.

3 Yarn over the hook, then work one chain stitch and tighten.

4 Completion of the 5-double crochet popcorn stitch (worked into a cluster).

Y-Shaped Stitch

  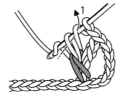  

1 Yarn over the hook twice, insert the hook into the back ridge of the chain, and work a treble crochet stitch.

2 Continuing, work one chain stitch, yarn over the hook, insert the hook into the 2 indicated stitches, yarn over, and pull through.

3 Yarn over again and pull through the 2 loops on the hook.

4 Yarn over once more and pull through the remaining 2 loops on the hook.

5 Completion of the Y-stitch.

✕ Crossed Double Crochet Stitch (yarn over twice for the first loop).

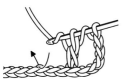 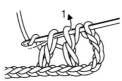   

1 Yarn over the hook twice, then work an incomplete double crochet stitch. Work another incomplete double crochet stitch into the indicated stitch.

2 Yarn over and pull through the two loops on the hook.

3 Yarn over and pull through two loops at a time.

4 Work two chain stitches. Yarn over, insert the hook into the two indicated stitches, and work a double crochet stitch

5 Completion of the crossed double crochet stitch.

✕ Crossed Treble Crochet Stitch (yarn over three times for the first loop).

 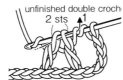  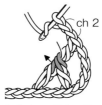 

1 Yarn over the hook 3 times, then work an incomplete treble crochet stitch. Work another incomplete treble crochetstitch into the indicated stitch.

2 Yarn over and pull through the 3 loops on the hook.

3 Yarn over and pull through 2 loops at a time.

4 Chain two stitches. Yarn over, insert the hook into the 3 indicated stitches, and work a double crochet stitch.

5 Completion of the crossed double crochet stitch.

⅄ Reverse Y-stitch (yarn over twice for the first loop).

  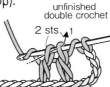  

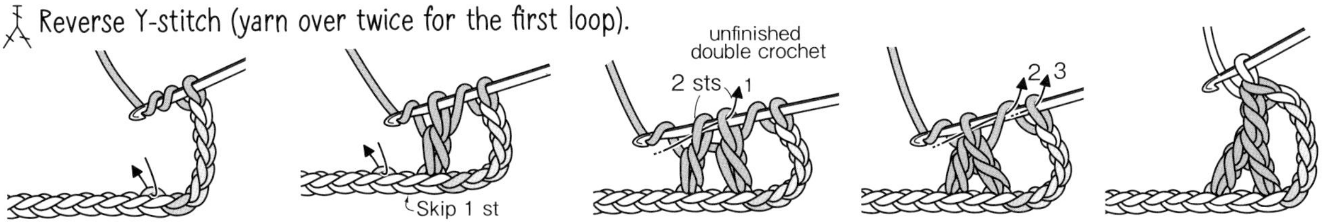

1 Yarn over the hook twice, insert the hook into the back ridge of the chain, and work an incomplete double crochet stitch.

2 Yarn over again, skip 1 chain, insert the hook into the back ridge of the next chain, work an incomplete double crochet stitch.

3 Yarn over and pull through the two loops on the hook.

4 Yarn over again and pull through two loops at a time.

5 Completion of the reverse Y-stitch.

� 5-Double Crochet Cluster Stitch

  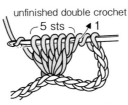  

1 Yarn over the hook three times, insert the hook into the back ridge of the chain, and work an incomplete double crochet stitch.

2 Yarn over the hook, work an incomplete double crochet in the same stitch, then crochet 4 more stitches.

3 Yarn over, and pull through the six loops on the hook.

4 Yarn over again, and pull through two loops at a time, twice.

5 Completion of the 5-double crochet cluster stitch.

🔺 Triangle stitch

1 Yarn over the hook five times, insert the hook into the back ridge of the chain, and work an incomplete quintuple treble crochet stitch.

2 Work an incomplete quadruple treble, followed by an incomplete triple treble, a double treble, and a treble in sequence.

3 Yarn over the hook and pull through the two loops on the hook.

4 Similarly, yarn over and pull through two loops on the hook twice, then pull through three loops on the hook.

5 Completion of the triangle stitch.

Tuva Publishing
www.tuvapublishing.com

Address
Merkez Mah. Cavusbasi Cad. No:71
Cekmekoy - Istanbul 34782 / Türkiye
Tel: +9 0216 642 62 62

366 Days Crochet Motifs

First Print
2024 / December

All Global Copyrights Belong to
Tuva Tekstil ve Yayıncılık Ltd.

Content
Crochet

English Edition

Editor in Chief
Ayhan DEMİRPEHLİVAN

Project Editor
Kader DEMİRPEHLİVAN

Tech Editor
Leyla ARAS

Graphic Designers
Ömer ALP
Abdullah BAYRAKÇI
Tarık TOKGÖZ
Yunus GÜLDOĞAN

All rights are reserved. No part of this
publication may be reproduced, stored
in a retrieval system, or transmitted in
any form or by any means, electronic,
mechanical, photocopying, recording, or
otherwise, without prior written consent
of the publisher. The copyrights of the
designs in this book are protected and
may not be used for any commercial
purpose.

ISBN
978-605-7834-86-7

TuvaPublishing

Edited by NIHON VOGUE Corp

AIZOBAN CROCHET MOTIF 366
KAGIBARIAMI PATTERN BOOK (NV70727)
Copyright © NIHON VOGUE-SHA 2023
All rights reserved.
Photographer: Yasuo Nagumo, Hidetoshi Maki
English translation rights arranged with
NIHON VOGUE Corp. through Japan UNI Agency, Inc., Tokyo